LITERARY CREATIONS

Conventional Characters in
the Drama of Shakespeare and
his Contemporaries

LITERARY CREATIONS

CONVENTIONAL CHARACTERS IN THE DRAMA OF SHAKESPEARE AND HIS CONTEMPORARIES

G. M. Pinciss

D. S. BREWER

© G. M. Pinciss 1988

First published 1988 by D.S.Brewer
an imprint of Boydell & Brewer Inc.
Wolfeboro, New Hampshire 03894-2069, USA
and of Boydell & Brewer Ltd
PO Box 9, Woodbridge, Suffolk IP12 3DF

ISBN 0 85991 267 1

British Library Cataloguing in Publication Data

Pinciss, G. M.
Literary creations : conventional characters
in the drama of Shakespeare and his
contemporaries.
1. English drama – Early modern and
Elizabethan,' 1500–1600 – History and
criticism   2. Characters and characteristics
in literature
I. Title
822'.3'0927   PR658.C47
ISBN 0-85991-267-1

Library of Congress Cataloging-in-Publication Data

Pinciss, G. M.
Literary creations.
Bibliography: p.
Includes index.
1. Shakespeare, William, 1564–1616 – Characters.
2. English drama – Early modern and Elizabethan,
1500–1600 – History and criticism.   3. English drama –
17th century – History and criticism.   4. Characters and
characteristics in literature.   I. Title.   II. Title:
Conventional characters in the drama of Shakespeare and
his contemporaries.
PR2989.P56   1988   822.3'3   88-2825
ISBN 0-85991-267-1

∞ Printed on long life paper
made to the full American Standard

Printed in Great Britain by
St Edmundsbury Press, Bury St Edmunds, Suffolk

Contents

Acknowledgments

Sections of this book have appeared earlier: a portion of Chapter II was published as an article, 'The Old Honor and the New Courtesy: 1 Henry IV,' in Shakespeare Survey 31 (Cambridge, 1978); and an earlier version of Chapter III was delivered as a paper at the Eighth International Conference on Elizabethan Theatre, Waterloo, Ontario. The conference papers were edited by George Hibbard and published as The Elizabethan Theatre VIII (Ontario, 1982). A part of Chapter IV served as the basis for a paper read in Lawrence, Kansas, at the Central Renaissance Conference in 1986. I am grateful for the permission to reprint here those portions of the book that first appeared under other auspices.

My research and writing have been greatly aided by a fellowship from the Huntington Library, San Marino, California; a sabbatical from Hunter College, City University of New York; and a grant from the George N. Shuster Fund at Hunter. In less tangible but no less crucial ways, I am deeply indebted to Professors Reg Foakes and Sam Schoenbaum for their encouragement, support, and example. Among my friends in the City University, Calvin Edwards and Mildred Kuner at Hunter have always offered valuable advice for which I am most grateful, and Richard Saez at Richmond College gave the entire manuscript a thorough reading; my work has profited greatly from their help. Above all, as in the past, two very dear friends have been essential for my sanity and resolve: without the patient kindness, critical judgment, and unfailing generosity of Marlies K. Danziger, my colleague and sometime collaborator, and the intelligence, perspicacity, and understanding of Dr Lewis W. Falb, Director of the Humanities at the New School for Social Research, this book – and much else – would be greatly diminished.

Perhaps I have taken his words too literally, but I could hardly find greater encouragement for this undertaking than the remarks of Professor Leonard Dean: 'In dealing with drama, the oldest and newest critics agree that it is best to start not with theory but with actual plays and learn about literature and life by attending to such practical things as stage types. ...' (Critical Inquiry, 1980)

For the faults and errors in this work I alone am responsible.

I

Introduction

Conventional characters – stock figures or stereotypes – have always been found in literature, for they offer particular advantages both to writers and audiences. For writers, stock characters are a kind of easy shorthand. They allow authors to jump right in, satisfying their eagerness to get on with plot and action, allaying their anxiety that their public will become bored with too much early description and analysis. Such stereotyped figures can be attractive to an audience as well: immediately recognizable, they usually call forth a simple, well-understood, and uncritical response. The least demanding of literary characters, they allow a story to get under way almost before we have met those involved in the plot.

In addition, stock characters offer special advantages to playwrights that should not be overlooked. Since such characters come prepackaged, complete with set personalities and motivations, they can be of special usefulness to dramatists, who work in a medium with more limited narrative possibilities as well as with more restricted length and scope than the novel. However, given careful and close attention, conventional characters may prove highly revealing. As a stock figure begins to differ from the standardized shapes and sizes of the norm, it can reflect changing social values. The stock figure, then, can reveal the distinctive qualities of an age, in particular the consequences of growing religious and ethical pressures on public attitudes.

The qualities we begin to detect in Renaissance conventional characters are in large measure a consequence of a new attitude toward the general notion of character itself, which is a product of Renaissance thinking. This new notion of character is suggested in the title of the second section of Jacob Burckhardt's great study of the civilization of the Renaissance in Italy, 'The Development of the Individual.'[1] According to Burckhardt, in

---

[1] According to Stephen Greenblatt in *Renaissance Self-Fashioning From More to Shakespeare*, pp. 161–162, Burckhardt 'remains one of the best introductions' to the development of the individual in the Renaissance. 'Burckhardt's crucial perception was that the political upheavals in Italy in the late Middle Ages, the transition from feudalism to despotism, fostered a radical change in consciousness: the princes and *condottieri*, and their secretaries, ministers, poets, and followers were forced by their relation to power to fashion a new sense

the Middle Ages, individuals derived their identity not from their own special qualities but from their membership in a group – whether race, people, party, family, or corporation. But with the Italian Renaissance, each person held a new consciousness of the self as a unique entity – a desire to express this individuality, unafraid 'of singularity, of being and seeming unlike his neighbours.'[2] Burckhardt believes this new way of thinking about oneself was a consequence of the political circumstances of the thirteenth century. But whatever the cause of this new awareness of self, it is an important distinguishing feature of the new age.

Once Renaissance man derived his own identity from traits of personality and behavior rather than from genealogy or from political or professional affiliations, the individuality of others also came to be defined by their temperament and action. Hamlet, for instance, tells Horatio that men's characters may be traced to one of three possible sources: their inherited nature – 'in their birth, wherein they are not guilty'; their temperament or disposition – 'By their o'ergrowth of some complexion' (i.e., the combination of the four elements in them); or, their customary pattern of behavior – 'by some habit.' Character, in other words, came to be determined by individual personality and conduct.

Yet, in fact, individual personality and conduct were generally reduced to rather rigid formulae. The four elements (earth, air, fire, and water) were thought to determine the four temperaments (melancholic, sanguinary, choleric, and phlegmatic), and the immutable laws of physiological psychology were held accountable for the humours of men. Still another law, that of decorum, derived from Aristotle, Cicero, Horace, and Quintilian, further limited the possibilities of speech and behavior. In Renaissance drama, according to Madeleine Doran, 'a certain type of person would be expected to do certain things, a certain passion to result in certain actions, and no explanation would be necessary.'[3] Perhaps the basis for classifying characters had changed somewhat from the Middle Ages and new categories were being added, but Renaissance dramatists were still working with stereotypes or stock figures.

Such stock characters have always been especially important in the drama, from the parasites and clever slaves of Roman comedy to the *pantalones* and *arlecchinos* of the *commedia dell'arte*, with their standardized action and dialogue. English Renaissance playwrights, too, used stereo-

---

of themselves and their world: the self and the state as works of art. But his related assertion that, in the process, these men emerged at last as free individuals must be sharply qualified. While not only in Italy, but in France and England as well, the old feudal models gradually crumbled and fell into ruins, men created new models, precisely as a way of containing and channeling the energies which had been released.'

2 *The Civilization of the Renaissance in Italy*, Vol. I, p. 144.

3 *Endeavors of Art: A Study of Form in Elizabethan Drama*, p. 251. See also Bridget J. Gellert, *Three Literary Treatments of Melancholy: Marston, Shakespeare, and Burton* for a discussion of a specific type, and Northrop Frye, *Anatomy of Criticism*, pp. 171–2 for some general remarks on the relation of stock characters to function and genre.

types, borrowing some directly from earlier writers; perhaps the braggart soldier, the *miles gloriosus*, is the best-known example.[4] But by the last quarter of the sixteenth century, dramatists in England had evolved their own distinctive and popular character types, figures such as the courtier, the savage man, the overreacher, the tool villain, and the shrew – the subjects of the chapters that follow.

Stock figures, such as those we shall consider, are often identified by their failings, a practice that may have been encouraged by the satirists. Hamlet, for example, tends to judge men in terms of their deficiencies, for he argues that behavior is very often determined by a 'particular fault':

> So, oft it chances in particular men
> That for some vicious mole of nature in them,
> . . .
> Carrying, I say, the stamp of one defect,
> Being Nature's livery or Fortune's star,
> His virtues else, be they as pure as grace,
> As infinite as man may undergo,
> Shall in the general censure take corruption
> From that particular fault. (I.iv.23–36)[5]

His rather jaundiced view of humanity is appropriate for a melancholic and disillusioned young man. But it is also a view reinforced by the 'satirical rogue' whose book Hamlet has been reading, one whose harsh descriptions of old age the Prince reports to Polonius (II.ii.). Indeed, the collections of satires, especially those written in bitter and ill-tempered verses, found a wide audience in the 1590s. Claiming the Latin satirists Juvenal and Persius as their Classical models, poets in the last years of the sixteenth century vied with one another to demonstrate their fury, contempt, and scorn of humanity. A slightly older generation of writers, Robert Greene in his cony-catching pamphlets of the early 1590s and Thomas Nashe in *Piers Penniless* (1591), had presented spirited and witty prose sketches of low-life types, and Thomas Lodge offered examples in both verse (*A Fig for Momus*, 1591) and prose (*Wits Miserie and the Worlds Madnesse*, 1596). But those who followed these writers, younger poets such as John Donne, Joseph Hall, and John Marston, were so extreme and libelous in their verses that by 1599 the publication of further satires was legally forbidden and a number of such works were burned.

After the turn of the century, collections of prose character sketches became popular with Joseph Hall's *Characters of Vertues and Vices* (1608), the first native English example of this genre. These 'characters' were a natural development from Elizabethan verse satires, but the form was actually influenced by its ancient Greek originator, Theophrastus, a contemporary

---

[4] This character has received especially thorough attention: see Daniel Boughner, *The Braggart in Renaissance Comedy*.
[5] I have used the Arden editions for all citations from Shakespeare's plays.

3

of Aristotle.[6] Theophrastus is credited with inventing the prose portrait, the presentation of a particular type whose behavior is 'dominated by a single vice. ... The result is the picture of a social type activated by a particular defect of character.'[7]

Hall in his 1608 book altered his Greek model by giving his sketches a moralistic purpose, adding portraits of virtuous types, and introducing a social context to his depiction of character. But the most successful and influential of these collections was started by Sir Thomas Overbury. The popularity of Overbury's writing was, no doubt, enhanced by the scandal surrounding his death by poison in the Tower, possibly at the instigation of the Countess of Essex. The Overburian character sketch improved on Hall's contribution to the genre by avoiding a moralistic emphasis and adding increasingly witty, conceited, and metaphoric language.[8] For Overbury, the prose 'character' describes the faults and virtues of a social type, complete with mannerisms and affectations. The twenty-two characters first published in 1614 were gradually increased in subsequent editions by 'other learned Gentlemen his friends' until a total of eighty-three sketches were included in the 1622 printing. Of these, some half dozen may have been added by Thomas Dekker and some twenty-two by John Webster. One can find in this collection a broad range of humanity: 'A Courtier,' 'An Affectate Traveler,' 'A Braggadochio Welshman,' 'A Puritan,' 'A Fair and Happy Milkmaid,' 'A Good Woman.'

Many of these satirists were playwrights – notably Greene, Nashe, Lodge, Marston, Dekker, and Webster. So the link connecting the satiric prose sketch to the character in a drama is easily traced: Nashe and Jonson, after all, were collaborators on The Isle of Dogs (1597), a play that angered both the Lord Mayor and the Privy Council. And as Jonson evolved the presentation of the humours characters, he created what has been called 'not a rounded portrait; not so much a man possessed by a quality as the quality itself embodied in the man.'[9] Jonson's brief analysis of the cast of Every Man Out of His Humour (1598), which he prefixed to the play, shows how greatly he was influenced by the character sketch:

> Puntarvolo. A vaine-glorious knight, over-Englishing his travels, and wholly consecrated to singularity; the very Jacob's staff of complement: a Sir that hath liv'd to see the revolution of time in most of his apparell. Of presence

---

[6] 'Although several editions of the Characters in Greek were published in the [sixteenth] century, "characters" on the Theophrastan model did not beome a literary vogue until after Causabon's Latin translation in 1592. What effect that vogue may have had on the increasing number of social types in Jacobean comedy is not easy to assess, for the influence may well have worked both ways, the writers of "characters" as freely borrowing from the dramatists as the other way about.' Doran, p. 228.

[7] The Overburian Characters by Sir Thomas Overbury, edited by W. J. Paylor, The Percy Reprints No. XIII, p. vi.

[8] Paylor, p. xiv.

[9] L. G. Salingar, 'The Elizabethan Literary Renaissance,' in The Age of Shakespeare, edited by Boris Ford, pp. 79–80.

good enough, but so palpably affected to his owne praise, that (for want of flatterers) he commends himself to the floutage of his own family. He deals upon returns and strange performances, resolving (in despite of public derision) to stick to his own particular fashion, phrase, and gesture.

Such concise, satiric prose 'characters' turn up not only where they may well be expected but often also where not:

Orl. I am he that is so love-shaked. I pray you tell me your remedy.
Ros. There is none of my uncle's marks upon you. He taught me how to know a man in love; in which cage of rushes I am sure you are not prisoner.
Orl. What were his marks?
Ros. A lean cheek, which you have not; a blue eye and sunken, which you have not; an unquestionable spirit, which you have not; a beard neglected, which you have not – but I pardon you for that, for simply your having in beard is a younger brother's revenue. Then your hose should be ungartered, your bonnet unbanded, your sleeve un-buttoned, your shoe untied, and everything about you demonstrating a careless desolation.

(As You Like It, III.ii.357–71)

Actually, we should expect dramatists to excel at writing the Over-burian-style sketch, for producing these thumbnail portraits that classify individuals by personality and behavior is a logical activity for playwrights. Although a sharp eye and a sensitive ear are essential to present characters on the stage through action and speech, what is even more important is the dramatist's ability to establish a recognizable type quickly. A novel has unlimited space in which to unfold many of the idiosyncrasies of those who live in its pages, but drama is a highly concentrated form, limited in duration, in narrative technique, and in stageable actions. As for its charac-ters, Renaissance playwrights had to create figures who are more than abstractions – those allegorical embodiments of the virtues and vices of Morality plays – but who are less than completely defined individuals.[10] Building character on the basis of widely accepted types provided the playwright with an essential shortcut to establishing the general shape and dimensions of his creations. For example, Hamlet is immediately identifi-able as a sufferer from that widespread, fashionable melancholy and mis-anthropy that afflicted many heroes of revenge plays and is subsequently found in the eponymous central figure of Marston's *The Malcontent* (1604) and Vendici in Tourneur's *The Revenger's Tragedy* (1606). But although Hamlet is a member of this generic family, he is denser, more complex, more mysterious than the others. As Eric Bentley has pointed out:

[10] 'The idea that all characters could be classified into "types" and their correct behaviour deducted from their types was due to the confusion of poetical and rhetorical theory which has been described so often. The sixteenth-century ideas of decorum were derived from Aristotle's *Rhetoric* and the *Characters* of Theophrastus; according to current interpretation it was wrong for a character to behave in any other manner than that proper to his type.' M. C. Bradbrook, *Themes and Conventions of Elizabethan Tragedy*, p. 56.

If the final effect of greatness in dramatic characterization is one of mystery, we see, once again, how bad it is for us, the audience, to demand or expect that all characters should be either predefined abstract types or newly defined concrete individuals. A mysterious character is one with an open definition – not completely open, or there will be no character at all, and the mystery will dwindle to a muddle, but open as, say, a circle is open when most of the circumference has been drawn. Hamlet might be called an accepted instance of such a character, for, if not, what have all those critics been doing, with their perpetual redefining of him? They have been closing the circle which Shakespeare left open. Which is not foolish, but very likely what Shakespeare intended. Foolish are only those critics who assume that the great geometrician would leave a circle open by accident.[11]

In the pages that follow we will explore the context – philosophical, social, historical – that helped define type characters and analyze those qualities and attitudes that are distinctive of each category. Each type character will be considered in relation to the intellectual currents that helped to shape it. Then, using one or more examples from Shakespeare's plays, each chapter will contrast his presentation of a specific type with those created by other Renaissance playwrights who wrote immediately before and after him. In this way we can hope to distinguish various embodiments of a type character and gain a sense of how and perhaps why the presentation of some type characters changed during this period. Each chapter will take up the plays it examines in chronological order.

The first chapter focuses on the ideal courtier. Using the advice on courtly behavior set forth by Sir Thomas Elyot and Castiglione, the authors of the two most important manner books of the Elizabethan-Jacobean period, we can compare the actions of Alexander the Great, the ideal hero of John Lyly's *Campaspe*, with three other spokesmen for differing views of the lifestyle of the perfect prince or courtier – Hal, Hotspur, and Falstaff in Shakespeare's *Henry IV, Part One*. Finally, we can compare Shakespeare's work with another that followed hard on its heels, Thomas Dekker's *Shoemaker's Holiday*. In this play, the king and the hero, Sir Rowland Lacy, embody strikingly different principles of courtly behavior from anything encountered in earlier examples.

Turning from one of the most civilized embodiments of humanity to one of the least, we shall next take up the type character of the savage man. Since this creature was most fully exploited by Spenser, we shall refer to *The Faerie Queene* to help identify three different subspecies of this genus, derived from a combination of classical literature, the folklore traditions of the English countryside, and the reports of travelers to the New World. The terrifying Bremo, the monster in the anonymous play *Mucedorus*, will be contrasted with Caliban in Shakespeare's *The Tempest*; Orson, the human child reared in the wild, one of the two brothers who are the heroes of another anonymous work, *Valentine and Orson*, will be compared with the abducted princes in Shakespeare's *Cymbeline*, who were brought up in the Welsh hills; and, finally, the behavior of the despondent Orlando

---

11 *The Life of the Drama*, p. 69.

in Robert Greene's *Orlando Furioso* will be considered as representative of a type of depressed madman dramatized also in Shakespeare's *Pericles* and *King Lear*. Like the courtier, the savage man can help define the role and value of civilization, in effect debating the old question of whether nurture is superior or inferior to nature. More interestingly, the savage man can also serve to define what separates the human from the animal, the man from the beast.

Chapter Three will discuss the overreacher, the hero who attempts to exceed the bounds of ordinary humanity. After reviewing something of his beginnings in classical mythology and in the late medieval drama as well as the impact of prevailing religious conceptions of humanity, we shall analyze Marlowe's Tamburlaine as the Renaissance prototype of the overreacher. Marlowe provides at least two influential versions of this figure, Tamburlaine and Doctor Faustus. Whereas Marlowe's treatments of the overreacher are generally serious, Jonson, writing more than twenty years later, turned the character from tragic hero to satiric butt, as can be seen in Sir Epicure Mammon in *The Alchemist*. Following in chronological order, we shall next consider Shakespeare's representative of this character type, the great hero-magician Prospero in *The Tempest*, who is, perhaps, the most complex and fascinating of overreachers. Finally, we shall examine Sir Giles Overreach, Massinger's Jacobean villain in *A New Way To Pay Old Debts*, whose very name announces his lineage.

The lowly agent of a Machiavel, the tool-villain, one who commits crimes that serve the interests of another, is the subject of the fourth chapter. Naturally, the writings of Machiavelli were held responsible for teaching what most men had always known. Perhaps the earliest tool-villain and surely one of the most straightforward can be found in Thomas Kyd's *The Spanish Tragedy*, and this example was soon followed by Marlowe's version of the type in *The Jew of Malta*. Shakespeare also presents several figures in this mold. Early in his career, in *Richard III*, he dramatizes through Buckingham a conventional representative of the role, but in the late romances, *Pericles* and *The Winter's Tale*, he looks more closely at the traditional figure of the tool-villain, exploring the ethical contradictions he embodies. In two later Jacobean tragedies the tool-villain, while still retaining his original function and identity, becomes even more altered. Both Webster in *The Duchess of Malfi* and Middleton and Rowley in *The Changeling* find ways of combining character growth and development with Jacobean sensationalism.

The last chapter will examine Renaissance attitudes toward the proper behavior of married women by comparing three presentations of the shrew. Ministers who sermonized on this subject offered a wide range of views, and many members of the clergy as well as the Anglican Church itself in its Homily on Marriage took quite precise yet varying positions. The authors of shrew-taming plays aligned themselves with one or another of these positions. The plays themselves are related, for the anonymous *The Taming of a Shrew* is directly connected with Shakespeare's *The Taming of the Shrew*, and John Fletcher's *The Woman's Prize, or The Tamer*

Tam'd was intended as a sequel to Shakespeare's work.

A close examination of these stock figures in the plays of Shakespeare and his contemporaries will enable us to recognize in specific and detailed ways how Shakespeare's treatment of the figures differs from that of his fellow playwrights and to identify what he particularly contributes to the gradual evolution of the types. Moreover, by selecting contrasting examples of a single character type from important works by major playwrights other than Shakespeare, we can increase our awareness of their plays, for as the practice of intertextual criticism repeatedly demonstrates, literary comparisons can prove enlightening.

Finally, by relating these stock figures to the intellectual currents of the period, we can more fully appreciate how their composition, evolution, and function were affected by contemporary thought. We shall find that comparing the ways in which Renaissance English playwrights dramatize conventional character types offers an especially rewarding means of recognizing what is distinctive about these writers or their material. Naturally, conventional characters must retain sufficiently similar outlines to be recognizable as belonging to an identifiable type. But over the course of time, the emphasis on specific individualizing qualities of type characters becomes gradually modified to reflect predominant cultural attitudes. As social values changed during the period under study, as the prevailing norms in ethics and morals, in religion, and in behavior became modified, so the presentation of what were traditional figures was affected as well. Clearly, the plays reflect the issues and approaches, the pressures of the age, and the audiences for whom they were written.

As we compare the treatment and presentation of these type characters in part to appreciate the shift in mood, the transition that was taking place in values, we should bear in mind that no single attitude or approach can be established as the cultural norm from which all else can be considered a variant. As several recent critics have pointed out:

> The dominant culture of a complex society is never a homogenous structure. It is layered, reflecting different interests within the dominant class (e.g. aristocratic versus a bourgeois outlook), containing different traces from the past (e.g. religious ideas within a largely secular culture), as well as emergent elements in the present. Subordinate cultures will not always be in open conflict with it. They may, for long periods, coexist with it, negotiate the spaces and gaps in it, make inroads into it, 'warrenning it from within.'[12]

The analysis of the philosophical, political, or cultural extremes illustrated by the behavior of each of the five chosen character types will provide us with a context for judging their actions and for gauging the extent of social change at the close of the sixteenth and in the early years of the seventeenth centuries.

[12] Tony Clarke, Stuart Hall, Tony Jefferson, and Brian Roberts, 'Subcultures, Cultures, and Class,' in *Resistance Through Rituals*, edited by Stuart Hall and Tony Jefferson (London, 1976), p. 12; the last quoted phrase is from E. P. Thompson's 'The Peculiarities of the English.' The entire paragraph is quoted by Alan Sinfield, *Literature in Protestant England 1560–1660*, p. 3.

II

The Courtier

The perfect prince or courtier, the young man whose future career involves a life at court and a devotion to political service, is an important character in Renaissance drama. When he is the hero of the work in which he
appears, his conduct usually defines the standards of proper behavior,
standards which seem to change radically in a very short period. To point
up how widely differing were the attitudes of dramatists in the closing
years of the sixteenth century, we shall compare three Elizabethan comedies: the earliest of the group, John Lyly's *Campaspe* (1584), sets forth the
manners, behavior, and goals considered proper for the ideal prince, the
youthful Alexander the Great. Next, in contrast, Shakespeare's *Henry IV,
Part One* (1597) offers an extensive comparison of various life styles and
patterns of conduct to consider what particular combination of traits
would best suit a future leader. And, finally, Thomas Dekker's *The Shoemaker's Holiday* (1599) proposes still another model of conduct as an ideal
for both prince and courtier.

Interestingly enough, Dekker's play was performed before Elizabeth on
the evening of January 1, 1600, 16 years to the day after Lyly's, and, if
rumors are to be trusted, since the Queen was so delighted by Falstaff that
she wished to see him in love, she must have watched Shakespeare's
trilogy on Prince Hal–Henry V. But the heroes of these works have more in
common than presentation at court. In each of them, the central character, tempted by pleasure, temporarily fails in his duty: Alexander and Sir
Rowland Lacy both succumb to the power of love, and Hal satisfies his
taste for a bohemian life style. At the conclusion we are led to believe that
all three heroes have accepted their destiny and will henceforth play a
responsible role in the political life of their country.

Consideration of a gentleman's manners, an analysis of those elements
of social conduct that are the most desirable aspects of a gentleman's
personality and character, was a popular concern in Renaissance England.
And of all the many Renaissance manuals on conduct, the two most
prominent Elizabethan guides to courtly behavior were Castiglione's *The
Courtier*, especially as translated by Sir Thomas Hoby in 1561, and that most

important of the English versions of Italian manner books, Sir Thomas Elyot's *The Governour* (1531).[1]

The approach and organization of the two works reveal their great differences. A staunch monarchist, Elyot sets out to define the obligations, moral and social, of those who hold public office. Dividing his study into three books, he first analyzes what education is appropriate to 'them that hereafter may be demed worthy to be governours of the publike weale.'[2] Elyot then discusses the attributes of character necessary for majesty and true nobility – such qualities as benevolence, affability, liberality and placability [easily forgiving]. And in the last book, he describes the moral principles that should govern conduct – such virtues as justice, faith, fortitude, patience, and magnanimity.

In contrast, Castiglione in *The Courtier* imagined a series of witty and sophisticated conversations based on his experiences in the cultured court of Urbino. In these talks, a distinguished gathering undertook 'to shape in wordes a good Courtier, specifying all suche conditions and particular qualities, as of necessitie must bee in him that deserveth this name.'[3] Although divided into four books, Castiglione's work focuses on the courtier primarily in Books I and II. In the first of these, the assembly describes the attributes, manners, abilities, and skills expected in one trained for a place at court – among these are noble bearing, good looks, courage, physical agility, fluency and polish in speaking and writing, knowledge of poetry, oratory, history, music, painting, and drawing, and, finally, skill as an amateur creator of the various arts. In the second book, the topic of conversation turns to the manner of the courtier's behavior, emphasizing the need for modesty, charm, spirit, wit, and a ready sense of humor, 'apt to all kinds of pleasantnesse.'[4]

The difference between these conduct books is even greater than such an overview suggests: for Elyot, serious dedication, strict application, and sound moral training form the basis of all the courtier's virtues; for Castiglione, style, as the manifestation of an inner refinement, is far more important. The Italian repeatedly stresses the essential quality of 'courtesie,' 'ease,' 'a certaine recklesnesse ... which augmenteth the grace of the thing,' accompanying 'all his doings, gestures, demeaners: finally all his motions with a grace.'[5] As Ruth Kelso has pointed out, something of a national character shaped the priorities of each writer: Castiglione and his countrymen, for example, stress personal and aesthetic matters; Elyot and

---

[1] See especially Ruth Kelso, *The Doctrine of the English Gentleman in the Sixteenth Century. The Governour* went through eight editions in its first fifty years, and, according to Kelso (pp. 118–119), *The Courtier* probably 'did more than any other one book to persuade the Elizabethan gentleman to unite learning to courtly graces.' Bibliographies can be found in Kelso, G. E. Noyes, *A Bibliography of Courtesy and Conduct Books in Seventeenth Century England* (New Haven, 1917), and Virgil B. Hetzel, *A Check List of Courtesy Books in the Newberry Library*.

[2] Edited by Henry Herbert Stephen Croft, Vol. I, p. cxcii.

[3] London, 1928, p. 29.

[4] P. 169.

[5] P. 43.

his readers place greater weight on civil usefulness and moral considerations.[6] Nevertheless, the two works have more in common than either shares with any medieval manual on knightly conduct; and, by and large, they agree on the manners that characterize a Renaissance gentleman.

Although an interest in defining the behavior and training necessary for true nobility remains strong throughout the late sixteenth century, the emphasis shifts during this period from Elyot to Castiglione, reflecting changes in public opinion. This shift in emphasis can be readily demonstrated in the theater where action and conflict combine to dramatize a philosophy of conduct. We can, perhaps, most readily appreciate how the stage can reflect this by turning first to the earliest work under discussion, *Campaspe*.

The main action of Lyly's play involves Alexander the Great's behavior in peace time: his dealings with philosophers and, especially, his falling in love with Campaspe, a captive 'borne of a meane parentage.' Gradually, the realization that Campaspe is an unsuitable mate in rank, that she is an unworthy goal for so great a man, and that she loves another, help Alexander regain his self-control. As the hero acknowledges at the conclusion: 'It were a shame Alexander should desire to commaund the world if he could not commaund himselfe.'

As the story is told in Book I of *The Courtier*, Alexander gives up Campaspe once he realizes he can never love her as much as the painter Apelles. According to Castiglione, artists such as Apelles, with their appreciation of beauty and their skill in representing it, will respond to true beauty with 'a farre greater delite' than any other man. And so, the painter having 'conceived a farre greater joye in beholding the beautie of Campaspe, than did Alexander, ... for this respect Alexander determined to bestow her upon him, that (in his mind) could know her more perfectly than he did.'[7] Castiglione's argument is lofty and idealizing, ennobling the sensitivity of the artist and elevating the power of love.

In contrast, the stage version of the story ignores the high motives for Alexander's conduct that Castiglione propounds. Rather than the values of *The Courtier*, Alexander in the theater acts on very different values that define for him the proper behavior of kings and those who serve them. In this case, the action tends to define honor in Sir Thomas Elyot's fashion, more through the duties and responsibilities of the ruler than through describing those graces that characterize Castiglione's prince. For example, in the dramatic treatment of the tale, Alexander relinquishes Campaspe largely because he comes to recognize his own obligations and limitations. Indeed, even the play's chaste and modest heroine is a very different creature from Castiglione's. According to Castiglione, Campaspe

---

[6] P. 50, p. 84.
[7] P. 82.

was 'sore agreeved to chaunge so great a king for a painter.'[8] But the heroine of the play has the good sense to fall in love with Apelles on her own and to realize that 'In kinges there can be no love but to queenes; for as neere must they meet in majestie as they do in affection.'[9]

This shift in Alexander's motivation allows the play to treat the question of honor by emphasizing the limits and responsibilities of rulers and statesmen rather than their manners and graces.[10] The action presents Alexander engaged in a series of conversations through which he begins to realize the duties and restrictions that come with power. And as these discussions proceed, this subject emerges as the central concern: the boundaries that an Alexander, committed to upholding his honor, must acknowledge before he can conquer the world – not what he may do only for recreation's sake. The play, then, stresses the limitations of power and emphasizes the need for self-knowledge and self-control to exercise such power honorably: *noblesse oblige*. Alexander clearly remains more a disciple of Elyot than of Castiglione.

In effect, the play achieves unity by presenting a sequence of interviews that with inexorable logic proves the limitations of even the most powerful ruler. For example, Alexander acknowledges that he may profit from philosophy – 'I have resolved with myself to have as many philosophers, as I had in my camp soldiers' – and he even accepts from Aristotle a premise that was, no doubt, close to the author's heart: 'nothing better becometh kings then [sic] literature.' But Alexander knows that if he is to rule successfully, matters of state must take precedence over the reasoning of intellectuals or the pleasures of fiction: 'in kinges causes I will not stande to schollers arguments.' Alexander recognizes, too, that what is appropriate and correct for others is not necessarily proper for him: Hephestion might prefer to 'leave war to studie wisdom' – and so might Alexander were he Hephestion. By the end of the first act, the youthful Alexander understands some of the burdens of his role.

In the remainder of the play, Alexander discovers how very limited his powers are. First, he confesses that he has fallen in love with Campaspe. His emotions are irrational, which explains how he has fallen in love with a woman unworthy of his affection; but since love is everywhere irrational, Campaspe cannot reason herself into loving Alexander and prefers the painter Apelles, who, it turns out, already loves her. Moreover, love cannot be commanded; even Alexander cannot order someone into reciprocating his love: 'I perceive Alexander cannot subdue the affections of men, though he conquer their countries.' Indeed, at an even more fundamental level, Alexander's earthly power has its limitations: he can-

---

[8] P. 81.

[9] P. 629.

[10] This reading differs from the two most extensive and rewarding discussions of the play. G. K. Hunter, *John Lyly the Humanist as Courtier*, p. 161, finds that the play debates the idea of true kingliness; Peter Saccio, *The Court Comedies of John Lyly*, p. 89, argues that 'the ruling idea of the play is not love. . . . The ruling idea is propriety, . . . the overwhelming importance of fulfilling one's rank.'

not alter such basic facts of life as birth and death or learn to paint with the talent of Apelles.

Born to conquer and rule, Alexander has passions greater than those of common men: 'none can conceive the torments of a king, unless hee be a king, whose desires are not inferior to their dignities.' But the hero soon recognizes the importance of recapturing his self-control: 'doubt not but Alexander can, when he wil, throw affections as farre from him as he can cowardise.' And with that remark near the end of the third act, Alexander begins to regain his sense of self and his sense of purpose. By the end of the play, he tricks Campaspe and Apelles into admitting their mutual love, and he announces he will return to his proper role as ruler and soldier. Henceforth, 'Alexander maketh but a toye of love, and leadeth affection in fetters, using fancy as a foole to make him sport, or a minstrell to make him merry.' Finally, at the conclusion, the play manages to restate the moral and still close the action on a gently mocking note:

Alex.   How now, Hephestion? Is Alexander able to resist love as he list?
Hep.   The conquering of Thebes was not so honourable as the subdueing of these thoughts!
Alex.   It were a shame Alexander should desire to commaund the world if he could not commaund himselfe. . . . And, good Hephestion, when al the world is woone, and every countrey is thine and mine, either find me out an-other to subdue, or, of my word, I wil fall in love!

Despite the occasional heavy-handedness of its treatment, *Campaspe* is a work of considerable charm and sweetness. These qualities are particularly unexpected in a play that insistently argues one must govern oneself in order to govern honorably and that finds the claims of duty are greater than those of personal satisfaction. Elyot surely would have approved of this message.

With this as its moral, *Campaspe* could hardly condone the freedom of conduct of later Renaissance courtly heroes. The strictness of Lyly's criteria for judging the behavior of rulers and the men about them barely allows for the kind of easy indulgence we are encouraged to extend to later truants from their obligations. The argument that greater familiarity with the ways of the common man will inevitably increase the humanity and the potential of a future ruler is an excuse never made by Alexander, whose views are clearly much more aristocratic. Instead, Alexander's behavior in love is presented merely as a brief, unproductive detour before he resumes what is for him the only honorable course of action – conquering the world:

Hep.   All these, Alexander, are to bee subdued – if that world be not slipped out of your head, which you have sworne to conquere with that hand.
Alex.   I confesse the labours fit for Alexander; and yet recreation [is] necessary among so many assaults, bloudye wounds, intollerable troubles. Give mee leave a litle, if not to sitte, yet to breath. And doubt not but

> Alexander can, when he wil throw affections as farre from him as he
> can cowardise.   (III.iv.)

These thoughts on conduct are as simple as they are charming – more simple even than what Elyot advocates in *The Governour*. As a character, the hero glimpses none of the complexity, ambiguity, and richness that make up the springs of human action nor does he seem to understand or appreciate the easy and graceful command of life that Castiglione's ideal prince demonstrates. The definition of proper behavior, as it is embodied in Alexander, is rigidly simple, clear-cut, and unmistakable.

The forthrightness of Lyly's approach is another mark of its simplicity: Alexander's reactions alone command our attention. Lyly develops no foil character to set off his hero's conduct. Yet that is exactly one of the means Shakespeare uses to enrich his treatment of this theme.

Written some dozen years after Lyly's play, *Henry IV, Part One* presents several rivals for our approval, all of them embodying differing principles of behavior. For example, central to any reading of this play is the dramatic opposition of the Prince of Wales with his arch-enemy Henry Percy: the frivolous, bored, and irresponsible behavior of Hal is set against the seriousness, energy, and courage of Hotspur. In large measure, these two young men, whom Shakespeare has intentionally portrayed as comparable in age, behave differently because they value differing codes of conduct. For Hotspur, honor, quite narrowly defined in military terms, is of over-riding concern. In this regard, he reminds one of Lyly's Alexander, duty-bound and determined above all to 'commaund the world.' Hal, however, acts as the chief spokesman for another virtue, one especially appropriate for a Renaissance prince: courtesy. By analyzing the actions of both men according to the advice of Elyot and Castiglione, we may arrive at a more precise evaluation of these two virtues and of those qualities that, it seems, ultimately mark Hal as superior to Hotspur.

Hotspur's behavior and ethics are intimately associated with the striving for honor. He is the 'king of honor'; according to the envious Bolingbroke, he is the 'son who is the theme of honor's tongue.' For him, public acclaim and reputation are to be earned chiefly by performance as a soldier – if not for, then against the crown. He is first mentioned at the very opening of the play in connection with a major victory over the Scots at Holmedon, and the impressive list of his prisoners is described to the king as an 'honourable spoil.' At his first appearance in scene three, Hotspur displays something of his warrior nature, for he is plain-dealing, quick-tempered, and fearless, all those traits common to the best Elizabethan soldier-stereotype; indeed, something of his nature can be found in such men as Kent, Enobarbus, and Othello. As Hal satirizes him, the young Percy 'kills me some six or seven dozen of Scots at a breakfast, washes his hands, and says to his wife, "Fie upon this quiet life, I want work."' There is more than a grain of truth in this exaggeration of Hotspur's aggressive determination.

Hotspur is also concerned with the king's treatment of his family since this, too, reflects on his honor. Bolingbroke's refusal to ransom Hotspur's brother-in-law Mortimer, to consult his father and uncle on matters of state, and to acknowledge the assistance of the Percys in taking the throne from Richard II are cited as particular reasons for rebelling. But all of these causes can be subsumed under one heading: his desire to 'pluck bright honor from the pale-faced moon.' For Hotspur this is the *summum bonum*.[11] Exasperated by Bolingbroke's tactics and encouraged to rebellion by his uncle, Hotspur in Act II no longer supports the crown against the Scots but joins them and the Welsh in an effort to unseat the king. He calls this 'so honorable an action,' an action by which his father and uncle 'may redeem your banished honors.'

Hotspur is not interested in material profit, as the action makes explicitly clear. In response to Sir Walter Blunt's hope that he will negotiate a peaceful settlement and accept an offer full of 'grace and love' from Bolingbroke, Hotspur answers, 'And maybe so we shall.' Indeed, Hotspur's motivation is so pure and his reply to Sir Walter so honest, that Worcester, Hotspur's uncle, never tells him of 'the liberal and kind offer of the king,' Bolingbroke's promise of amnesty. Worcester persuades his companion, Sir Richard Vernon, perhaps wisely, that his nephew must never learn what Bolingbroke promised. Unlike the open and rather naive and gullible Hotspur, Worcester truly understands that the politic Bolingbroke knows 'at what time to promise, when to pay.' But actually, Hotspur's honesty and directness, although laudable and appealing to us, are not entirely praiseworthy traits for one who hopes to gain a place at court. To attain the kind of influence Hotspur is seeking, both craftiness and calculation are occasionally excusable practices.[12]

In truth, as a Renaissance courtier Hotspur is inept. The play systematically dramatizes his failures in the many skills, talents, and graces that every sixteenth-century nobleman should exhibit. The deficiencies in Hotspur's nature are repeatedly displayed to the audience not only by his own actions but also by pointed comment from others. In his very first speech he confesses to the court that he answered the king's messenger 'neglectingly, I know not what ... for he made me mad.' Although his conduct might be excusable in special circumstances, it is hardly correct or controlled behavior. Hotspur then proceeds to contradict Bolingbroke flatly, not using Touchstone's Retort Courteous nor the Quip Modest, but the Counter-check Quarrelsome and the Lie Direct. Men of good sense would stop short of such an offensive reply – from which there is no retreating without an 'if.' Bolingbroke in fury orders the Percys away. Finally, unable to control his anger, Hotspur cannot allow his uncle to hold the floor without behaving like a 'wasp-stung and impatient fool.' All this in the opening scene! Surely we are watching a young man lacking in

---

[11] See Curtis Brown Watson, *Shakespeare and the Renaissance Concept of Honor*, p. 66ff.
[12] Watson, p. 67.

patience, moderation, and prudence, those virtues Elyot thought so essential in one who looked for a place at court.[13]

Like Elyot, Castiglione, too, would have observed several deficiencies in Hotspur's behavior. His impetuous nature and quick tongue are obvious liabilities at the council table, but in the pleasures of civilized life he is equally undeveloped and uninterested. Glendower, the Welsh chieftain, boasts that he has composed English lyrics, 'a virtue that was never seen' in Hotspur. But the younger man has no shame at his deafness to the beauties of language:

> I had rather be a kitten and cry 'mew'
> Than one of these same meter ballad-mongers.
> I had rather hear a brazen canstick turn'd
> Or a dry wheel grate on the axle-tree,
> And that would set my teeth nothing on edge,
> Nothing so much as mincing poetry.   (III.i.123–128)

Obstinate in his ways, he takes delight neither in verse nor in music. A lady's song is a subject for teasing his wife, and a lullaby in Welsh is less pleasing to him than the howling of his Irish wolf-hound; presumably neither the music nor the language hold appeal. Had he followed the advice of Castiglione, Hotspur would have known how untutored was his insistence on knowing 'onely the nobleness of armes.' A true courtier should

> exercise him selfe in Poets, and no lesse in Oratours and Historiographers, and also in writing both rime and prose, and especially in this our vulgar tongue. For beside the contentation that hee shall receive thereby him selfe, hee shall by this meanes never want pleasant intertainements with women which ordinarily love such matters.

And like the great warrior Achilles, taught to play the harp by Chiron, a soldier is no less heroic for his talent with music. Castiglione insists that such skill is not effeminate: 'musicke is not an ornament, but also necessarie for a Courtier.'[14]

Hotspur's weaknesses are more than implied. His failures and his faults are named by his uncle lest we overlook them. Although Worcester may not appear the ideal teacher, his experience at dealing with men is unquestionably greater than his nephew's and his admonition is worth heeding. He criticizes Hotspur for his blunt and sarcastic treatment of Glendower, whom they hope to make an ally in their planned rebellion against Bolingbroke:

> You must needs learn, lord, to amend this fault.
> Though sometimes it shows greatness, courage, blood –

---

[13] Kelso notes, p. 76, that Elyot and his successors 'in general cover the same ground' in their descriptions: 'The virtues that were by common consent considered the most important for the gentleman were justice, prudence, courtesy, liberality, temperance, and fortitude.'

[14] P. 71, p. 77.

And that's the dearest grace it renders you –
Yet oftentimes it doth present harsh range,
Defect of manners, want of government,
Pride, haughtiness, opinion, and disdain,
The least of which haunting a nobleman
Loseth men's hearts, and leaves behind a stain
Upon the beauty of all parts besides,
Beguiling them of commendation.   (III.i.174–183)

The charges Worcester recites sum up a rather complete bill of particulars against Hotspur. But there still remains at least one fact about the young man's attitude that shows to what extent it is uncharacteristic of his time. When he learns that his father is unable to bring his support to the confrontation with Bolingbroke, Hotspur argues that 'It lends a larger dare to our great enterprise.' When he learns that Glendower, too, will be unable to join them, Hotspur still insists on rushing into battle. His courage and enthusiasm are admirable; his eagerness to encounter an enemy who vastly outnumbers him – 'Die all, die merrily' – reveals the extent of his idealism. But rushing into battle, rejoicing to display bravery, enduring suffering and loss or even meeting death gladly as a reward for valor are the actions of a medieval knight demonstrating the code of chivalry. Such deeds are not those of a Renaissance gentleman; the ideal performance of a crusader in a romance is not the same as that of a courtier in a sixteenth-century manners book, and the behavior of a hero in a tale by Malory hardly agrees with Castiglione's recommendation:

it is behovefull both for himselfe and for his friends, that he have foresight in the quarrels and controversies that may happen, and let him beware of the vantages, declaring alwaies in everie point both courage and wisedom. Neither let him runne rashly to these combats … for beside the great daunger that is in the doubtful lot, he that goeth headlong to these things deserveth great blame.[15]

On this issue of heroism in battle, the career of the Douglas, Hotspur's Scots ally, offers a telling contrast. Before the fighting begins at Shrewsbury, Hotspur praises him as the best of soldiers, 'a braver place/ In my heart's love hath no man than yourself.' And, indeed, the Douglas urges a speedy confrontation with Bolingbroke, actively seeks him in battle, and systematically attempts to kill each of those dressed like the king. His fight with the real king, however, is interrupted by Prince Hal, who comes to aid his failing father. Rather than meet death at Hal's hand, the Douglas flees. Then we learn that the noble Lord Douglas

when he saw
The fortune of the day quite turn'd from him
The noble Percy slain, and all his men

[15] P. 40. For further discussion of this point, see Kelso, p. 93. Shakespeare is not everywhere consistent: before the battle of Agincourt, Henry V argues like Hotspur that greater glory is gained by fighting when one is greatly outnumbered.

> Upon the foot of fear, fled with the rest,
> And falling from a hill, he was so bruis'd
> The pursuers took him.   (V.v.17–22)

The misfortunes of the Douglas are Hal's opportunity to demonstrate the nobility of his own spirit. The Prince instructs his brother John to free the imprisoned enemy leader without ransom, for

> His valors shown upon our crests today
> Have taught us how to cherish such high deeds
> Even in the bosom of our adversaries.   (V.v.29–31)

That Hal would commit a public act reflecting what Prince John calls 'high courtesy' is not unlikely, but that Hal would praise for his courage a rebel who ran away when he saw defeat and death approaching is a little startling if one considers what Hotspur might have said had he seen it all. From all of this we can only conclude that Hotspur's values are not the same as those of his enemies or his friends, for unlike him both Hal and the Douglas approve of that advice that teaches one to flee when one is outnumbered or outclassed.

Hotspur's chief virtue – and he is called the 'king of honor' by the Douglas – is defined by a code of manners that is obsolete; he represents an age that is past or passing. Prince Hal, on the other hand, embodies the new virtues: even before he inherits the kingdom from his father he is dubbed the 'king of courtesy.'[16]

Courtesy, Hal's most distinctive attribute, is considered by both English and Italian authorities a necessary quality for a nobleman's temperament, one so central that Spenser devoted a whole book of The Faerie Queene to it. Courtesy is exercised by knowing what is fitting for oneself and others, and for enacting this with graciousness.[17] One's conduct, then, is affected in part by an awareness of class differences and the lines between classes, and in part by the desire to draw praise and admiration for the manner of one's behavior, especially from one's equals and betters. Such a person in Elyot's terms possesses 'a gentil and familiare visage' able to procure men's love, and 'a beautie or comelynesse in his countenance, language, and gesture apt to his dignitie, and accomodate to time, place, and company.'[18] When the waiters at the Boar's Head dub Hal the 'king of courtesy' and promise he 'shall command all the good lads of Eastcheap,' the Prince of Wales has proven something of his real worth. He is both truthful and slyly ironic when he says to Poins, 'thou hast lost much honor that thou

---

[16] For Shakespeare, the question of gentility or true nobility was more than a literary topos. He himself had applied to the College of Heralds at about the time he was composing this play for his family's coat of arms. Despite the fact that the College was held in poor repute by the end of the sixteenth century, Shakespeare evidently accepted the popular notion that no one was a gentleman unless he was registered there. For further remarks on the College of Heralds see Kelso, p. 25ff.

[17] Kelso, pp. 79–80.

[18] P. 131; p. 121.

wert not with me in this action.' Drinking-deep and sounding the very bass string of humility are evidence of princeliness, for Hal has followed Castiglione's injunction:

> in companie with men and women of al degrees, in sporting, in laughing, and in jesting, he hath in him certaine sweetnes, and so comely demeanours that who so speaketh with him, or yet beholdeth him, must needes beare him an affection for ever.[19]

In fact, Hal satisfies most of Castiglione's criteria for courtesy: he is noble by birth, witty by nature, comely in person and countenance, and attractive with 'a certaine grace and (as they say) a hewe, that shall make him at the first sight acceptable and loving unto who so beholdeth him.'[20] These aspects of courtesy are perhaps more gifts of nature than manners consciously learned and artificially cultivated, but such gifts, as one might expect, are part of the legacy of a royal offspring.

Recognizing Hal's natural courtesy and his supremacy in this virtue allows us to reinterpret the claims of others. For example, Hotspur's threat that Hal will 'shrink under my courtesy' seems a hollow boast when one realizes Hal's true value, and so Bolingbroke's criticism of Hal's conduct should also be regarded with some skepticism. Bolingbroke has 'majesty,' the quality that impresses his public; but this is only half of what Elyot finds necessary for courtesy. The king never gains his public's affection, lacking what Elyot would have called 'affability,' the other component of courtesy. In fact, Bolingbroke is a fraud; like Macbeth in borrowed robes, he 'dressed' himself in humility to pluck allegiance from men's hearts, and 'stole all courtesy from heaven.' His rebuke to his son, a parallel to Worcester's reprimanding Hotspur, reflects only Bolingbroke's own obtuseness. Even Sir Richard Vernon, who could scarcely be expected to think favorably of Bolingbroke's heir, appreciates Hal's innate graciousness of manner and speech. He describes to Hotspur how the Prince delivered his offer of single combat:

> I never in my life
> Did hear a challenge urg'd more modestly,
> Unless a brother should a brother dare
> To gentle exercise and proof of arms.
> He gave you all the duties of a man,
> Trimm'd up your praises with a princely tongue,
> Spoke your deservings like a chronicle,
> Making you ever better than his praise
> By still dispraising praise valu'd with you,
> And, which became him like a prince indeed,
> He made a blushing cital of [reference to] himself,
> And chid his truant youth with such a grace

[19] P. 33.
[20] P. 33.

As if he mastr'd there a double spirit
Of teaching and of learning instantly.

(V.ii.51–64)

From Vernon's account it is clear that Hal can act with modesty, ease, and charm. He seems to embody the characteristics that Castiglione found in the young Ippolito d'Este, Archbishop of Ferrara and friend of Ariosto and Leonardo:

> He hath so happie a birth, that his person, his countenance, his words, and all his gestures are so fashioned and compact with his grace ... that a man would weene he were more meete to teach, than needfull to learne.[21]

Indeed, the Prince's challenge to fight Hotspur alone, made before the leaders of the opposing parties, is in accordance with Castiglione's precepts for winning 'most estimation' in time of war; Hal's proposal is effective in 'separating him selfe from the multitude' and in offering to 'undertake notable and bolde feates.'[22] The challenge itself is phrased with such humility and filled with such self-criticism and self-awareness that Hal's own nature seems unassuming and gracious. Harry Percy is described as a paragon of the age:

> I do not think a braver gentleman,
> More active-valiant or more valiant-young
> More daring or more bold, is now alive
> To grace this latter age with noble deeds.

And of his past conduct, Hal can only pretend to be embarrassed:

> For my part, I may speak it to my shame,
> I have a truant been to chivalry,
> And so I hear he doth account me too.   (V.i.89–96)

The modesty and dignified language of Hal's proposal – 'to save the blood on either side,/ Try fortune with him in a single fight' – recalls Castiglione's description of how the ideal courtier would address his audience. Such a man's words reveal:

> a simplicitie of such meekenesse of minde, that a man would weene nature her selfe spake to make them tender and (as it were) dronken with sweetnes; and with such conveyance of easinesse, that who so heareth him, may conceive a good opinion of him selfe and thinke that he also ... mighte attaine to that perfection.[23]

That he is 'facile or easie to be spoken unto' by all except poor Francis, the puny drawer, who can barely speak at all, is half of Hal's attraction; the other half is his talent for speaking 'courtaisely, with a swete speche or countenance, wherwith the herers (as it were with a delicate odour)

[21] Pp. 32–33.
[22] Pp. 95–96.
[23] P. 57.

be refressed, and alured to love him in whom is this most delectable qualitie.'[24]

Even what appear to be Hal's failings must be reconsidered by the criteria for behavior that Castiglione and Elyot describe: one should not expect that all Hal's vices will metamorphose into virtues, but at least the mold of form will be defined by the expectancy of the time. Bolingbroke and Hotspur criticize Hal for his friends: he has acted like a 'sword and buckler Prince of Wales' and has 'mingled his royalty with capering fools.' But both Hal's critics are unsympathetic to the importance of public affection, and, as we have noted, both are out of touch with the advice published in the best Renaissance guides. Castiglione, for example, believes if 'the Courtier in jesting and speaking merry conceites have a respect to the time, to the persons, to his degree, and not use it too often ... hee may be called pleasant' and a man of humor.[25] That Hal knows something of this is clear when in the last act he scolds Falstaff for his impertinent answer to Bolingbroke's question about the reasons for the rebellion, or again, when Hal on the field of battle asks his fat friend rhetorically, 'What, is it a time to jest and dally now?' Perhaps Hal is excessively given to the frivolous, but even his taste for practical jokes merits some approval: according to *The Courtier* 'a merrie prancke is nothing else, but a friendly deceite in matters that offend not at al or very little.'[26]

Hal's worst faults can actually be used to display the basic goodness of his nature. Elyot illustrates the importance of placability by relating the story of Hal, the madcap prince, and the Chief Justice who put him in prison. By obeying the court, Hal

> a prince and sonne and heire of the kynge, in the middes of his furye, more considered his ievall example, and the juges constance in justice, than his owne astate or wilfull appetite. ... Wherefore I conclude that nothing is more honorable, or to be desired in a prince or noble man, than placabilitie.[27]

Finally, Hal's horsemanship symbolizes his prowess as a Renaissance prince, for it offers the most hyperbolic image of the wastrel turned courtly hero in the play. On horseback he emerges completely cleansed from the stain of riot and dishonor. Appearing as Bellerophon, glittering in a golden coat, Hal rises 'from the ground like feather'd Mercury,/ And vaulted with such ease into his seat/ As if an angel dropp'd down from the clouds/ To turn and wind a fiery Pegasus,/ And witch the world with noble horsemanship.' Such skills as Hal exhibits he might have practiced at the recommendation of either Elyot or Castiglione. Elyot endorses the ability 'to ryde surely and clene on a great horse and a roughe' as 'the most

---

[24] Elyot, p. 130.
[25] P. 168.
[26] P. 170
[27] Pp. 140–141.

honorable exercise, in myne opinion, and that besemeth the astate of every noble persone.'[28] *The Governour* also commends as 'a right good exercise which is also expedient to lerne, whiche is named the vauntinge of a horse: that is to lepe on him at every side without stirroppe or other helpe, specially whiles the horse is goinge.'[29] For his part, Castiglione would have a Courtier 'a perfect horseman for everie saddle. And beside the skill in horses ... let him set all his delight and diligence to wade in everie thing a little farther than other men' while accompanying 'all his motion with a certaine good judgment and grace.'[30]

To sum up this argument, we discover that judged by the standards of conduct recommended in *The Courtier* and *The Govenour*, the two most influential manners books in sixteenth-century England, Hal is not truly a wastrel nor Hotspur a paragon. In fact, the behavior of the Prince at Shrewsbury and even his subsequent career as king are a consequence of the further development of those character and personality traits that Castiglione and Elyot considered essential for success. Indeed, Hal, as one of England's greatest rulers, ought properly to embody those talents and skills the Elizabethans looked for in the best representatives of nobility. Hotspur's absolute candor, straightforward honesty, and indominable determination are not such virtues after all, it seems, just as Hal's deviousness – 'I know you all' – truancy, and self-indulgence may be signs that anticipate desirable princely traits.

In the case of Hal and Hotspur we have seen to what a great extent their public behavior attempts to conform to a socially accepted, even idealized notion of human conduct. As a consequence, when the two ultimately meet at Shrewsbury, we witness the inevitable clash between the 'king of honor' and the 'king of courtesy.' But these young men who follow opposing philosophies of conduct nevertheless share a significant quality: they both demonstrate powerful political ambitions, their self-interest is combined with a commitment to government and power that is the spur to all their actions. In this way the self-interest of Hal and Hotspur is similar

[28] P.78.

[29] P.79.

[30] P.41. A general discussion of Shakespeare's indebtedness to Castiglione, Elyot, and Lyly will be found in E. M. W. Tillyard's *Shakespeare's History Plays*, pp.314–318. Tillyard points out that *Henry V* has often been interpreted as 'a quasi-Aristotelian paradigm of the theme of honour. ... Hotspur, the argument goes, represents the excess, Falstaff the defect, and Hal the virtuous mean of the honourable man.' See also Norman Council, *When Honour's At the Stake*, p.136 and his citations in footnote 1, p.57. Council, in fact, argues that Hal is a pragmatist rather than an embodiment of an Aristotelian mean. A. R. Humphreys in the Arden edition of *Much Ado About Nothing* argues that the influence of *The Courtier* on this play, written at about the same time as *Henry IV*, was very strong, providing Shakespeare with 'patterns of courtesy and wit.' p.15ff. Humphreys also discusses Shakespeare's indebtedness to Lyly's style, p.19, 25–26, and Appendix II. Emrys Jones in *Scenic Form in Shakespeare* argues that Shakespeare was highly familiar with and influenced by Lyly's *Campaspe*, pp.239, 243.

and differs from the kind of self-interest we find in Falstaff.

In his candor, Falstaff never conceals his dedication to hedonism. Eating, drinking, and wenching are his pursuits; thieving his means. Yet, however much this life-style suits Hal's fat old friend, the world can never condone his behavior. Accordingly, he acknowledges the need for redemption – again and again:

> *Now am I, if a man should speak truly, little better than one of the wicked. I must give over this life, and I will give it over. (I.ii.)

> *Well, I'll repent, and that suddenly, while I am in some liking. I shall be out of heart shortly, and then I shall have no strength to repent.
> (III.iii.)

> *I'll purge, and leave sack, and live cleanly, as a nobleman should do.
> (V.iv.)

But this promised change to a better life is never accomplished. Unlike Hal, who not only swears to reform but also demonstrates his reformation on the battlefield, Falstaff, the old reprobate, is incapable of change. He can believe in nothing but himself, and his philosophy of conduct is guided by his appetites. In the conflict between honor and courtesy, then, Falstaff serves to undercut both these principles of behavior. For him Hal's 'courtesy' comes to be seen as merely a dignifying label, enabling the heir apparent to indulge in a pattern of behavior that is as self-interested as Falstaff's own. And in Falstaff's eyes, Hotspur's 'honor' turns him into a power-hungry rebel who would seize the crown just as Bolingbroke had done. Despite what men say, they are moved in Falstaff's view by what is beneficial to themselves: 'Rebellion lay in his way, and he found it' is his flippant explanation for Worcester's action. We dignify our deeds by giving them names that disguise the personal profit that truly motivates them: 'Honor is a mere scutcheon.' Yet, of course, Falstaff's unqualified enjoyment of life, his energy, wit, and inventiveness, soften this cynicism. He can treasure humanity at the same time that he holds no very high opinion of it. He has made a total commitment to self alone.

Our reaction to Falstaff, the irrepressible, and to his life style is most strongly affected by the way he fulfills – or fails to fulfill – his role as army captain, leading a troop of infantry soldiers. Familiar with 'all the poor abuses of the time,' Falstaff first chooses to draft those who can buy out their military service. (Although not for sale by a captain, such exemptions could legally be purchased for 40 shillings, a sum beyond a poor man's savings.) Then, Falstaff pockets these fees, although for this practice officers were subject to a fine of ten times the sum taken.[31] Having im-

---

[31] P. A. Jorgensen, 'Military Rank in Shakespeare,' *HLQ*, 14 (1950), I:17–41. According to Jorgensen, p. 30, 'Falstaff's behavior is so accurately opposed to that recommended for captains that it might serve as a model in reverse for the precepts of military conduct books.' See also *Shakespeare's England* on 'The Soldier' by G. W. Fortescue, pp. 112–113.

pressed a troop of hardened convicts and tattered prodigals into service, he is at once callous and accurate in his assessment of the military strength of the company he leads: 'good enough to toss; food for powder; food for powder. They'll fill a pit as well as better.' In the battle he makes his prediction come true by leading his men to their death: 'There's not three of my hundred and fifty left alive, and they are for the town's end, to beg during life.' And, of course, he will continue to draw the pay of those no longer able to collect it themselves.

These contrasting philosophies of conduct, old-fashioned honor, new-fangled courtesy, and timeless hedonism, are adeptly balanced. We can enjoy Falstaff for his wit and his fundamental honesty. In Hotspur's case, his over-commitment to a misguided ideal is tempered by his youth, his impatience, and his ingenuousness. Finally, in the courteous prince we find a young man responsive, affable, and almost too clever, entirely capable of growth and development, of learning that combination of skills necessary for the successful ruler.

A very different view of conduct appropriate for the courtier and the prince is shown in Thomas Dekker's *The Shoemaker's Holiday*. Dekker's work was written very soon after Shakespeare completed his three plays with Hal as hero, and *The Shoemaker's Holiday* was directly influenced by Shakespeare's trilogy. Simon Eyre, the shoemaker who becomes Lord Mayor of London, one of Dekker's most colorful creations, was not a little affected by Falstaff's hearty blustering, and the unnamed English king who appears victorious from France at the conclusion of this work seems modeled on Shakespeare's own Henry V.

Although *The Shoemaker's Holiday* follows in the footsteps of Shakespeare, it is very different in genre and in point of view. Dekker has chosen to create a romantic comedy rather than a chronicle history, and he has understood that the conventions governing such comedies may legitimately demand elements of the sentimental and improbable. Moreover, the social values of *Shoemaker's Holiday*, the definitions implied for such concepts as 'honor' and 'courtesy,' are far less sophisticated, serious, and coherent than those we found in *Henry IV, Part One* and far less aristocratic and duty-bound than those in *Campaspe*.

Dekker adapted two of the three strands of his plot from Thomas Deloney's *The Gentle Craft*.[32] The story line that is used with least alteration dramatizes Simon Eyre's rise from shoemaker to Lord Mayor.[33] The

[32] A full discussion of sources will be found in the Revels edition of R. L. Smallwood and Stanley Wells, p. 17ff.

[33] Yet, as Alexander Leggatt points out in *Citizen Comedy in the Age of Shakespeare*, p. 19, even in this borrowing the changes are not without significance. 'Eyre makes his fortune by a commercial venture, buying a cargo of merchandise from a Dutch skipper, which he is able to resell at a handsome profit to himself. Dekker is at pains to assure us that Eyre is not cheating

second related action, which required greater changes in setting and characterization from the original source, involves the love affair of Sir Rowland Lacy, the nephew to the aristocratic Earl of Lincoln. Lacy disguises himself as a Dutch shoemaker in order to woo Rose, the daughter of a staunchly middle-class father, Sir Roger Oatley. The last of the three story lines, the impressment of the poor shoemaker Ralph and his separation from and reunion with his wife Jane, Dekker fashioned wholly out of traditional materials. With excellent craftsmanship Dekker interconnected all three of these episodes: Lacy and Ralph are employees of Eyre's; Lacy's knowledge of languages helps Eyre begin his rise to wealth and fame; and Hammon, an unsuccessful rival suitor, courts first Rose and then Jane.

Moreover, all three story lines are united by the same sentimental world view. Unlike Shakespeare's and Lyly's plays, Dekker's work argues for a false egalitarianism, and its presentation of moral behavior involves no greater ideals than money, work, and love – in that order.[34] Not simply its language, but the shallowness of its moral judgment sharply distinguishes Shoemaker's Holiday from the other plays we have examined.

The case for equality among the classes is restated constantly. It is, in fact, one of the points stressed by the action of the play. For example, even the king himself, in an act as questionable as it is romantic, endorses the misalliance of Lacy and Rose with the argument that 'love respects no blood.' And Simon Eyre lends his support to this democracy of spirit by repeatedly announcing to the world: 'Prince am I none, yet am I nobly born, as being the sole son of a shoemaker.' To keep class distinctions a subject of mockery, Eyre's wife, Margery, is teased and berated for her haughty manners and condescension. Significantly, this failure to support class distinctions leads ultimately to the dissolution of those concepts of honor and courtesy encouraged by Castiglione. The connection is not hard to find: accepting one's membership in a particular class means fulfilling the responsibilities expected of the members of that class. But in a classless society individuals are free from social pressure; they can ignore duties and obligations that they accepted earlier as a part of a code of conduct which proved they belonged to a particular class.

---

the skippper, for the transaction takes place on the latter's own suggestion. The affair is curiously underplayed: the relevant action takes place offstage, and we are given only the meagre details about it. Dekker's departure from his source is significant, for it involves the (I think) deliberate suppression of material. In Deloney ... Eyre indulges in a bit of subterfuge. ... He even disguises himself. ... Dekker, in order to show Eyre as an example to proper social behaviour, is more careful than Deloney to keep his hero, in the eyes of the audience, innocent of greed or guile.'

[34] According to Leggatt, the play uses 'the conventional devices of comedy as vehicles for social analysis' (p. 32), the action demonstrating 'that prosperity must be linked with generosity, not only in the golden world of civic legend but in the world of hard reality as well' (p. 20).

This disapproval of class distinctions is presented in a highly biased and inconsistent manner.[35] As a citizen of London, Ralph, the shoemaker, who has neither wealth nor title, is impressed into military service and must leave his wife of less than a year to serve as a soldier. But Lacy, the aristocratic gentleman, appointed by the King 'chief colonel of all those companies/ Mustered in London and the shires about/ To serve his Highness,' never leads his troops. In his place, Lacy sends his cousin Askew and remains behind to woo Rose. Instead of agreeing that Lacy might be justly criticized, if not punished for his actions – in his anger, Lacy's uncle quite rightly calls him 'traitor' – the king in the best romance fashion grants Lacy pardon: ''Twas not a base want of true valor's fire/ That held him out of France, but love's desire.' But in concluding the romantic plot with an arbitrary happy ending, Dekker reduces the hero's character. Lacy's marriage to Rose does not actually cross class boundaries because Lacy is, in truth, no gentleman at all. His vows are never to be trusted. He swears to his uncle, the Earl of Lincoln:

> I will for honour – not desire
> Of land or livings, or to be your heir –
> So guide my actions in pursuit of France
> As shall add glory to the Lacy's name. (Sc. i.86–89)

But the moment Lincoln departs, Lacy bribes Askew to assist him in his scheme. And later in the same scene Lacy confirms just how casually he gives his word when he consoles the unhappy Ralph with a promise of his assistance, a promise he has already arranged to break: 'Give me thy hand./ Thou shalt not want, as I am a gentleman.' Even Falstaff never lies so convincingly to himself. The discrepancy between Lacy's language and his conduct reveals how shallow is his definition of 'honourable' or 'gentlemanly' behavior. Yet self-interest and self-concern are hardly seen by him as deficient motives for conduct. And this fact explains why, unlike Hal on the one hand or Falstaff on the other, Lacy has no speech acknowledging that his behavior requires both an admission of wrongdoing and a demonstrated reformation. Rather the King, who claims to believe that love comes before all, compensates Lacy's in spite of his obtuseness:

> As for the honour which he lost in France,
> Thus I redeem it: Lacy, kneel thee down,
> Arise Sir Rowland Lacy. (Sc. xxi.113–115)

The king as *deus ex machina* in this story also provides the resolution for the class conflict between Rose's father and Lacy's uncle. Both parent and guardian scarcely conceal from each other their mutual distrust and dislike under a strained *politesse*. Oatley argues that the extravagant living of a

---

[35] For a discussion of the ambiguities and inconsistencies between Dekker's comedy and the competitive commercialism of the play see Joel H. Kaplan, 'Virtue's Holiday: Thomas Dekker and Simon Eyre,' *Renaissance Drama* N.S. II (1969), 103–22, and Peter Mortenson, 'The Economics of Joy in *The Shoemaker's Holiday*,' *SEL*, 1976, 16:241–52.

nobleman such as Lacy would destroy his finances: 'Too mean is my poor girl for his high birth./ Poor citizens must not with courtiers wed.' In truth, Oatley is contemptuous of the life style of the aristocracy and encourages Rose to marry a man such as Hammon, 'a proper gentleman,/ A citizen by birth, fairly allied.'

And Oatley's low opinion of the aristocracy, barely concealed from Lincoln, is the perfect counterpart for Lincoln's own low opinion of the bourgeoisie. He, too, would prohibit the marriage between Lacy and Rose, 'whose mean birth will much disgrace his bed.' In fact, Lincoln's opposition to the marriage is even greater than Oatley's: 'I do mislike the match far more than he./ Her blood is too, too base.'

Again, King Henry resolves all differences under love's banner: 'Dost thou not know that love . . ./ Cares not for difference of birth or state.' And once again, the happy ending, arbitrarily imposed, provides no suggestion of a changed attitude in the unhappy father or the angry earl. The king's romantic ruling does not alter the truth of the class conflict, for the play does not dramatize the serious social and moral questions it raises; these issues are suppressed in the noise of celebrating. True love, good cheer, and universal fellowship are presented as the strength of English society. As Alexander Leggatt says, one will not find 'any serious social thinking' here.[36]

This analysis is, perhaps, rather hard on *The Shoemaker's Holiday*, but unlike the plays of Lyly and Shakespeare it seems on the whole unconscious of the larger issues it raises. Dekker's play points out some of those elements that are increasingly altering the nature of English society, yet with characters who can provide neither intellectual nor philosophical insight, we are asked to believe that friendship, geniality, and a harmless jingoism can cure all. The more disturbing or inconsistent actions of character and plotting are concealed by clever craftsmanship – for example, we never actually see Eyre disguised as an alderman pretending to have the capital to pay for the merchandise that leads to his financial success. Indeed, the whole matter of his fraudulant business scheme is quite quickly glossed over.

In fact, *The Shoemaker's Holiday* has provided a glimpse into the not-too-distant future. In that new age, the social and moral responsibilities defined by the traditional class structure will break down as the old aristocracy is supplanted by the 'new men' who will rise to wealth and power under King James. Despite its enforced jollity, *The Shoemaker's Holiday* foreshadows the end of the old Elizabethan social contract.

The self-indulgent and socially irresponsible behavior of Sir Rowland Lacy joined with the complicity of the king in rewarding this conduct suggests that the action of future heroes is not to be judged by the rigid

---

[36] P. 80. 'Simply stated, the play depicts the victory of individuality over class, of honesty over affectation, of good fellowship and love over divisiveness and war.' *Revels* edition, p. 31.

standards of Alexander or the more varied and politically subtle criteria of Hal. (We should recall that Shakespeare's king would not spare Bardolph from hanging in order to ingratiate the English invaders with the French.) Whether a man can escape military duty and injury, or whether, like poor Ralph, he may return home from the wars a cripple and nearly lose his wife is purely a matter of money and position. This code of behavior endorses personal and material success as a substitute for social achievement and spiritual attainment. *The Shoemaker's Holiday* lacks the wit, style, and bite of the comedies that held the stage at the close of the seventeenth century, but its hero's morals foreshadow those of the rakes who might well have learned a thing or two about irresponsibility and self-indulgence from him.

III

The Savage Man

A reader of English Renaissance pastorals will quickly discover that the savage man is a frequently met inhabitant of that literary landscape, almost as often encountered as the shepherds and aristocrats one expects to find there.[1] In large measure, the savage man's usefulness to Renaissance poets and playwrights explains his popularity, for he can function both as an entertainer, merely a figure of ridicule, and as a philosophic symbol. Indeed, when considered seriously, the savage man can raise a number of profound and intriguing questions, complex issues which have no simple answer: is 'civilized' man truly superior to natural man, or is man reared in a state of nature superior to man brought up in society? Or, to put it another way, is heredity (i.e. 'nature') more important in determining the character of an individual than education or training (i.e. 'nurture' or 'art')? Beyond this, the savage man as a stage figure can demonstrate whether savages can be socialized or whether they benefit from socialization. Finally, at the most fundamental level of all, the figure of the savage man enables a thoughtful writer to ask what ultimately separates man from the animals and on what basis such a distinction can be drawn. Man, after all, can degenerate into the bestial just as he can in his conduct imitate the angelic. In short, the character type of the savage man provides far more than a focus for the great Renaissance debate over the superiority of art over nature, or nature over art.

The scope and the various questions raised about the nature of humanity by this stage character can be analyzed by considering examples in two anonymous plays, *Mucedorus* (1590) and *Valentine and Orson* (1595), as well as those in Robert Greene's *Orlando Furioso* (1591) and Shakespeare's *The Tem-*

---

[1] The following works offer especially useful discussions of the pastoral: John Arthos, *On the Poetry of Spenser and the Forms of Romance*; Donald Cheney, *Spenser's Image of Nature: Wild Man and Shepherd in the Fairie Queene*; Rosalie Colie, *Shakespeare's Living Art*; Patrick Cullen, *Spenser, Marvell, and Renaissance Pastoral*; Walter R. Davis, *Sidney's Arcadia*; Howard Felperin, *Shakespearean Romance*; R. G. Hunter, *Shakespeare and the Comedy of Fogiveness*; Frank Kermode, ed. *The Tempest*; Maynard Mack, *King Lear in Our Time*; Edward Tayler, *Nature and Art in Renaissance Literature*; Humphrey Tonkin, *Spenser's Courteous Pastoral*; David Young, *The Heart's Forest and Something of Great Constancy: The Art of 'A Midsummer Night's Dream'*.

pest (1611), *Cymbeline* (1609), *Pericles* (1608), and *King Lear* (1605). In addition, to help classify the various types of savage men and understand the characteristics that distinguish them, we shall refer to Spenser's *The Faerie Queene* (1590; 1596) for a preliminary description of each of the three types of savage men we shall examine most closely. This approach will enable us not only to distinguish among each type but also to contrast how a similar figure was used by writers of subtlety and genius as well as by those endowed with more modest gifts.

The savage man could trace his ancestry back both to classical mythology and to European folklore.[2] From classical mythology the Renaissance learned of Romulus, who was reared by a she-wolf; of Hercules, the friend of man, who dressed in a lion's skin and carried a club; and of satyrs, fauns, and sileni, who existed in a Golden Age and a state of innocence. These were positive examples of kindly and beneficent creatures living happily in accord with nature. They represented the 'soft' view of primitivism formulated by Hesiod, described by Ovid's Golden Age, and championed by Locke, by Rousseau and, most recently, by Levi-Strauss.

The opposing point of view held that primitive existence was truly bestial and that society, through collective effort and human reason, was the only means of improving the quality of life. The savage man's constant struggle for survival, his unrestrained response to physical desires, his brutal existence in a world of fallen nature explained his violent, lascivious, unpredictable, and even cannibalistic behavior. Ironically, the same examples served: Romulus murdered his brother; Hercules went mad; and satyrs and fauns, creatures of prodigious sexual capacity, worshipped Bacchus in frenzy. This line of reasoning represents the 'hard' view of primitivism, expressed by Lucretius and argued in the Renaissance by Machiavelli as well as later by Hobbes and Freud.

In addition to a Classical ancestry that provided both positive and negative qualities, the Renaissance savage man derived a part of his lineage from an equally ambivalent medieval folklore. By the early Middle Ages citizens of Italy, France, and Switzerland could be terrorized by rumors of a forest-dwelling wild folk living in a state of nature.[3] These savages were associated with demons of the earth as well as with ghosts of the underworld and were thought of as enemies of living things and of man himself. Another strain, encountered with only slightly less fear, was associated with the elves and fairies of country lore, impish, not always kindly, and connected with vegetation and fertility.[4] By the High Middle Ages, however, attitudes had shifted. The frustration caused by a rigid, elaborate, and artificial code of courtly manners precluding spontaneity of

---

[2] Hayden White, 'The Forms of Wildness: Archaeology of an Idea,' in *The Wild Man Within*, edited by Edward Dudley and Maximillian Novak.

[3] Richard Bernheimer, *Wild Men in the Middle Ages*.

[4] See for example, *Robin Goodfellow; his mad prankes and merry jests* (1628) and R. A. Foakes, introduction to *A Midsummer Night's Dream*.

expression and denying natural conduct led men to long to escape the repressions of society, to live unrestrained in nature. Accordingly, the wild man became a model for human conduct, a creature free, happy, and loving.

Perhaps the most influential writer of the English Renaissance who made the most comprehensive use of the Savage Man was Edmund Spenser. In Book I of The Faerie Queene, for example, he introduces a 'salvage nation' who live at ease in nature, creatures who may well be described as free, happy, and loving. They are capable of recognizing the holiness of Una and protecting her, even if they cannot correctly comprehend her notion of the true faith. But unlike them, their relations in Book III are not herbivorous; a goat-herding tribe, this lot is most remarkable for its unrestrained sexuality. With bagpipes, dances, and garlands they celebrate the arrival of the strumpet Hellenore. Finally, in Book VI, the unfortunate virgin Serena is captured by still another bagpipe-playing 'salvage nation,' one that does not practice trade, 'drive/ The painefull plough, or cattell for to breed/ ... But on the labours of poore men to feed.' And, as it turns out, they feed on poor men themselves, for, once they have seen Serena, 'of her dainty flesh they did devise/ To make a common feast.' Depending on the needs of the allegory and the choice of genealogy, Spenser created savages of every description.

In this matter of description we may be, at first, somewhat surprised at the identification of the savage man with creatures that are at least half-beast. But the wild man as a gentle or beneficent creature of the forest was not very different, after all, from those other inhabitants of woods and streams, the satyrs, fauns, nymphs, and sileni of classical mythology. Bernheimer in his study of the wild man in the Middle Ages notes that by the twelfth century 'the wild man himself is given the traits of a satyr' – hairiness, strength, virility, semi-nakedness, and aphasia.[5] Moreover, as Hayden White has pointed out, the positive revaluation of the image of the wild man as a benign creature occurred simultaneously with the 'recovery of classical culture, the revival of humanist values, and the improvisation of a new conception of nature more classical than Judeo-Christian in inspiration.'[6] By the early Renaissance all human and even semi-human creatures of the forest were simply thought of as savages or wild men, whatever their origin.

Like their mythological and medieval antecedents, the accounts of voyagers to the New World were also frequently an ambiguous and often downright contradictory source for images of the savage man. James Rosier's Diary of a trip along the Virginia coast in 1605 illustrates how changeable were a European's notions of the American natives. On his first meeting with the savages on 30 May, his reaction was highly favorable:

[5] P. 99.
[6] Pp. 22–23.

They seemed all very civill and merrie: showing tokens of much thankeful-nesse, for those things we gave them. We found them then (as after) a people of exceeding good invention, quicke understanding and readie capacitie.[7]

But after some further contact with the Indians, Rosier quickly changed his mind. His diary entry four days later, on 3 June, reveals how poor a reputation the Indians had among the English and how suspicious and distrustful the explorers soon became. Arriving where they had agreed to exchange furs and skins, the English discovered an assembly of some

> two hundred and eight-three Salvages, every one his bowe and arrowes, with their dogges, and wolves which they keepe tame at command, and not anything to exchange at all; but would have drawen us further up into a little narrow nooke of a river, for their Furres, as they pretended. These things considered, we began to joyne them in the ranke of other Salvages, who have been by travellers in most discoveries found very trecherous; never attempting mischiefe, untill by some remisnesse, fit opportunity affordeth them certaine ability to execute the same.[8]

John Smith's view of the American native is also harshly negative. After his sixth voyage to Virginia (1607–1609), Smith described the inhabitants as:

> inconstant in every thing, but what fear constraineth them to keepe. Craftie, timerous, quicke of apprehension, and very ingenuous. Some are of disposi-tion fearefull, some bold, most cautelous, all Savage. Generally covetous of Copper, Beads, and such like trash, they are soone moved to anger, and so malicious that they seldome forget an injury: they seldome steal one from another, least their conjurors should reveale it, and so they be pursued and punished.[9]

Unlike these explorers, some philosophers held very different opinions of the character of the inhabitants of the New World. Montaigne argued in the essay 'Of Cannibals' that man in primitive society has a direct, natural simplicity and vigor which in European man has been 'bastardized' by the 'corrupted taste' of a sophisticated and artificial culture. That explorers and essayists express such antithetical views must reflect not only per-sonal experience but also the attitudes and preconceptions about the natural life held by the writer himself.

Perhaps the most basic presentation of the savage shows him as the least human and most bestial creature. In Spenser's treatment, he displays the

---

[7] *A Tryue Relation of the most prosperous voyage made this present yere 1605, by Captaine George Waymouth, in the Discovery of the land of Virginia: Where he discovered 60 miles up Written by James Rosier, a Gentleman employed in the Voyage* (London, 1605), pp. 21–22.

[8] Pp. 34–37.

[9] From *The Second Book: The Sixth Voyage to Another Part of Virginia* in *The Generall Historie of Virginia, New England and the Summer Isles* (London, 1624), p. 66.

usual characteristics of his kind – he is strong, speechless, armed with an oak tree, covered in hair, and dressed with a wreath of green ivy – there is nothing attractive in his person:

> It was to weet a wilde and salvage man,
> Yet was no man, but onely like in shape
> And eke in stature higher by a span,
> All overgrowne with haire, that could awhape
> An hardy hart, and his wide mouth did gape
> With huge great teeth, like to a tusked Bore
> For he liv'd all on ravin and on rape
> Of men and beasts; and fed on fleshly gore,
> The signe whereof yet stain'd his bloudy lips afore.
>
> (IV. vii.)

His resemblance to humanity is hard to find: his head bears a pouch-like nether lip, a 'huge great nose ... empurpled all with bloud,' and 'wide, long eares ... More great than th'eares of Elephants.' As the distraught Amoret learns, this creature makes a speciality of women: 'For on the spoile of women he doth live,' and 'with his shamefull lust doth first deflowre,/ And afterwards themselves doth cruelly devoure.' Since sexual potency is a common attribute of the species, this 'wilde and salvage man' functions as the embodiment of uncontrolled sexuality.[10]

Among the earliest examples of this same type of savage to appear in the drama is Bremo, who made the anonymous play *Mucedorus* both thrilling and delightful to many Elizabethans. In fact, Bremo is quite possibly the most popular and long-lived of his species on the public stage, a figure no doubt familiar to Spenser, Shakespeare, and their audience. Bremo displays all the signs of his class:

> With restless rage I wander through these woods;
> No creature here but feareth Bremo's force,
> Man, woman, child, beast, and bird,
> And everything that doth approach my sight
> Are forced to fall if Bremo once do frown.
>
> (vii.)

But having captured the Princess Amadine, he finds that his own fierceness is mollified by a new emotion; he discovers that 'her beauty hath bewitched my force/ Or else within me altered nature's course.' Where he had first thought to 'feed on flesh' and 'glut' his 'greedy guts with lukewarm blood,' he is now overcome with love. This new sensation causes

---

[10] See James Nohanberg, *The Analogy of the Fairie Queene*, p. 256n. for an analysis of this creature's appearance. My colleague Calvin Edwards has pointed out to me that Spenser's association of the figure of lust with 'a tusked Bore' refers perhaps to the interpretation of the boar as destructive lust in some of the allegorized readings of Ovid's story of Venus and Adonis.

him to recite what passes for the best lyric poetry in the play – 'pastoral' in style:

> The satyrs and the wood-nymphs shall attend on thee
> And lull thee asleep with music's sound,
> And in the morning when thou dost awake,
> The lark shall sing good morrow to my queen,
> And, whilst he sings, I'll kiss my Amadine.   (xv.)

That Amadine can retain her chastity must be proof of the strength of her influence over Bremo and the degree of his love for her. The power of love is further tried when she persuades Bremo to spare Mucedorus, the prince who loves her. Mucedorus explains to Bremo that his life style is barbaric and uncivilized, that a 'goodly golden age' could be achieved when men led by reason 'grew to perfect amity,' forsaking the woods and living in cities and towns. Nevertheless, Mucedorus agrees to serve as Bremo's servant while 'the monster ... doth murder all he meets;/ He spareth none, and none doth him escape.' In short order, however, Mucedorus tricks Bremo into giving him a club and with that 'strikes him down dead.'

What distinguishes Bremo are his fierceness and bluster, his credulity and guilelessness, his susceptibility to love, and his unexpected gift for lyricism. Despite what must have been a threatening appearance on stage – his 'huff, snuff, ruff' speeches are comically cruel – Bremo is very much a child, willful, innocent, and subject to extreme rage. Unlike Spenser's incarnation, Bremo has nothing of the sinful or wicked about him. He functions in this plot purely as an exciting but temporary obstacle to the happy ending.

Shakespeare's presentation of a Bremo-like savage, Caliban, offers far greater subtlety and complexity. Although this creature in The Tempest is in many ways strikingly different from all other varieties, that he shares some of Bremo's characteristics is hardly surprising. In a revival of Mucedorus, Bremo, after all, had appeared before King James in a performance acted by Shakespeare's company at about the time The Tempest was itself being composed for court presentation.

Caliban is described in the First Folio list of characters as 'salvage and deformed.' His ancestry and the long-established tradition for presenting him on stage are well suggested by Edmund Malone's note on his costume: Caliban's dress 'which doubtless was originally prescribed by the poet himself and has been continued, I believe, since his time. [This] is a large bear skin, or the skin of some other animal; and he is usually represented with long shaggy hair.' [11] However, that he is compared by

---

[11] The Tempest edited by Frank Kermode, p. 63. As Rosalie Colie has noted, 'The satyr-figure, half-animal, half-human, sometimes represents disorder and danger in the pastoral world and at other times exhibits heightened pathos. The ambiguity of this type is very important in aspects of Caliban's presentation.' Shakespeare's Living Art, p. 258, ft. 4.

Trinculo and Stephano to a fish and associated with fishiness must attest rather to his strangeness and to his smell than to his derivation. Like Bremo, Caliban is both threatening and comic, and like him also he has learned speech. In addition, he, too, is capable of a lyric outburst:

> the isle is full of noises,
> Sounds and sweet airs, that give delight, and hurt not.
> Sometimes a thousand twangling instruments
> Will hum about mine ears; and sometimes voices,
> That, if I then had wak'd after long sleep,
> Will make me sleep again; and then, in dreaming,
> The clouds methought would open, and show riches,
> Ready to drop upon me; that, when I wak'd,
> I cried to dream again.   (III.ii.133–141)

How Bremo acquired language is not explained, but Caliban had the advantage of Miranda's instruction. As she reminds him:

> [I] took pains to make thee speak, taught thee each hour
> One thing or other: when thou didst not, savage,
> Know thine own meaning, but wouldst gabble like
> A thing most brutish, I endow'd thy purposes
> With words that made them known.   (I.ii.356–360)

Perhaps among her lessons she also converted Caliban from cannibalism; as we have seen, this was a practice common among his ilk and one, as his name suggests, that had not always been alien to him. Finally, he exhibits the last of the major qualities of the wild man in his lusting for Miranda and in his near success at peopling the isle with little Calibans.

Although 'savage and deformed,' Caliban has more subtle reactions and emotions than his predecessors in part because his origins are more complicated. He is not simply a wild, two-legged creature, but the offspring 'got by the devil himself' upon a witch. And combined with his supernatural parentage, his heredity also includes an historical element, for Shakespeare has made his savage a native inhabitant of the New World. Caliban might be found both among the cannibals and in the Caribbean.[12]

Perhaps this more complex derivation accounts for some of the imaginative and psychological complexity of Caliban. For example, denied the pleasure of Miranda's bed and forced to serve Prospero's will, Caliban expresses a very human bitterness over lost love: 'When thou cam'st first,/ Thou strok'st me, and made much of me ... and then I lov'd thee,/ And show'd thee all the qualities o' th' isle.' That he is capable of such affection is unusual, and that he is capable of improvement through instruction indicates a nature far above that of the earlier breed of savage men.

---

[12] Kermode, p. xxxviiiff. See also Charles Frey, 'The Tempest and the New World,' Shakespeare Quarterly (Winter, 1979), 30:29–41; John E. Hankins, 'Caliban and the Natural Man,' PMLA (1947), 62:793–801; and G. Wilson Knight, 'Caliban as a Red Man,' in Shakespeare's Styles, edited by P. Edwards, I.-S. Ewbank, and G. K. Hunter.

Since his behavior is uncontrolled, purely id-directed, and since he has never attained an understanding of any moral code, he is truly beyond good and evil. His intention of murdering Prospero is restrained by fear not of damnation but of detection and punishment. Moreover, he has the sense not to be distracted from his purpose with 'trash,' as are Stephano and Trinculo.

But, in fact, Caliban's attempt would fail even if it were to succeed; he would merely replace one master with another. His efforts to attain freedom are misdirected. The lesson that Ferdinand expresses, that fulfillment of the will comes through submission of the will, that freedom is found through restraint, is a paradox too subtle for Caliban – at least before the very ending of the play. Only in his last speech does Caliban acknowledge his foolishness and announce 'I'll be wise hereafter,/ And seek for grace.'

According to Frank Kermode, 'Caliban is the ground of the play.'[13] And, indeed, to every character and thread of the action he provides a point of contrast. He is a servant who wants his freedom; Ariel is another. But Caliban is composed of the low and heavy elements, earth and water, while Ariel is all fire and air. Caliban is deformed and lustful, one who cannot be made to bear logs without the threat of punishment; Prince Ferdinand, on the other hand, is one of the handsomest of his kind, who accepts his log-bearing as the imposition of 'poor matters' for 'rich ends.' Ferdinand's desires can never 'melt . . . honour into lust.' Between the two we are presented with the opposition of self-restraint with lawlessness, of self-control with willful behavior. And, since Caliban is motivated by lawlessness and lust, he has proved largely unresponsive to Prospero's efforts:

> Thou most lying slave,
> Whom stripes may move, not kindness! I have us'd thee,
> Filth as thou art, with human care; and log'd thee
> In mine own cell, till thou didst seek to violate
> The honour of my child. (I.ii.346–350)

Even the very words Caliban has learned are turned to curses in his mouth. He seems the product of forces forever in opposition to those higher powers, civilizing and refining, of Prospero's art.

In the action of the play, Caliban's resentment at his treatment by Miranda and her father leads him to encourage Stephano and Trinculo to aid in the murder of Prospero and to set themselves up as lords of the island. Caliban's efforts parallel the temptation of Antonio, who encourages Sebastian to murder his brother and make himself the King of Milan. Antonio, after all, knows this practice well, for he has succeeded in supplanting Prospero, his own brother, as Duke of Naples.

---

13 P. xxv.

Yet here we begin to realize that what had seemed clear-cut distinctions between the civilized and the savage no longer hold. In fact, the more closely we examine the play, the more deceptive is its simplicity. Caliban is, it seems, a part of all of us, even the most rarified examples. Prospero himself admits: 'this thing of darkness I acknowledge mine.' And we must balance Prospero's discouragement with Caliban – 'He is one on whom my nurture would never stick,' 'He is one on whom my pains are all lost, quite lost' – with Caliban's own closing comment that he will 'seek for grace.' Even to acknowledge its desirability suggests that Caliban is a savage capable of humanity, a possibility expressed by Gonzago, that old man who makes a practice of being right in essence while being wrong in detail:

> If in Naples
> I should report this now, would they believe me?
> For I should say, I saw such islanders, –
> For, certes, these are people of the island –
> Who, though they are of monstrous shape, yet, note,
> Their manners are more gentle, kind, than of
> Our human generation you shall find
> Many, nay, almost any.   (III.iii.27–34)

Moreover, Caliban has the wit to repent as well as the sense to seek improvement. Sebastian and Antonio, men who commit evil in full knowledge of their wickedness, never sue for forgiveness or promise reformation. And this points to the ultimate paradox of The Tempest: that the savage in his uncivilized amorality may indeed be potentially more human than some of civilization's most aristocratic products; that, in the final analysis, Caliban may prove Antonio, the European, the more savage creature. Breeding may be an insufficient basis on which to predicate conduct. As Miranda wisely observes, 'Good wombs have borne bad sons.'

The Tempest is indeed a play rich and strange. Even Montaigne in his delightful essay 'Of Cannibals,' which Shakespeare probably enjoyed, did not push cultural relativism this far. Caliban's potential for growth and development comes as something of a surprise, even though the turn of events is entirely appropriate in a play about forgiveness, redemption, and reformation. Still, we hardly expect to find Caliban portrayed in a way that suggests his superiority to European aristocracy, for one of the principal tenets of the pastoral convention was the inherent virtue of class and breeding. Even when their experiences have been confined to sheep and pastures, the truly noble will reveal themselves. Pastorella and Perdita are two exemplary figures of this kind, and the hero of As You Like It, denied the education and society appropriate for one of his blood, nevertheless re-mains 'full of noble device.' Caliban serves to raise one's doubts about all this.

Renaissance writers were well aware that another type of wild man, a more noble savage, could make just the point that good breeding predisposed one to virtue. In this case, too, models can be found in Spenser and pre-Shakespearean drama. As Amoret's captor in Book IV of *The Faerie Queene* and Bremo in *Mucedorus* represent for us the savage savage, so Spenser's 'Salvage Man' in Book VI and Orson in the anonymous play *Valentine and Orson* exemplify the gentle or noble variety.

Spenser's noble savage arrives on the scene attracted by the cries of Serena and Sir Calepine.[14] This 'Salvage Man' defends them against the attack of Sir Turpine, whom he puts to flight. Spenser's creation is fearless and invulnerable, though without needful vestments or language. Yet he is skilled in the medicines of the forest, capable of pity, gentleness, 'deepe compassion,' and even a kind of reason. Living only on the nourishment of wild fruit, he 'neither plough'd nor sowed,/ Ne fed on flesh, ne ever of wyld beast/ Did taste the bloud, obaying natures first beheast.' His sympathy for the wounded lady as well as his regard for her safety and respect for her chastity indicate that

> though he were still in this desert wood,
> Mongst salvage beasts, both rudely borne and bred,
> Ne ever saw faire guize, ne learned good,
> Yet shewd some token of his gentle blood,
> By gentle usage of that wretched Dame.
> For certes he was borne of noble blood,
> How ever by hard hap he hether came,
> As ye may know, when time shall be to tell the same.   (VI.v.)

Although Spenser unfortunately never completed the story of the Salvage Man, a self-contained incident that the poet combines with the Salvage Man's history offers an indirect comment on it. This short episode involves Sir Calepine's rescuing an infant from the mouth of a bear and bestowing the baby on the childless Lady Mathilde. As Sir Calepine points out, in this infant, whatever his real parentage, the adopting parents

> may enchace
> What ever formes ye list thereto apply,
> Being now soft and fit them to embrace
> Whether ye list him traine in chevalry
> Or noursle up in lore of learn'd Philosophy.   (VI.iv.)

In Spenser's notion of child development, heredity is important but environment plays a major role as well:

---

[14] For background, see Roy Harvey Pearce, 'Primitivistic Ideas in the *Fairie Queene*,' *JEGP* (1945), 44:139–51. A rewarding discussion of the themes raised here will be found in Tonkin, p. 58ff. and Cheney, especially p. 209ff.

> certes it hath oftentimes bene seene,
> That of the like, whose linage was unknowne,
> More brave and noble knights have raysed beene,
> …
> Then those, which have bene dandled in the lap.   (VI.iv.)

The two stories taken together reflect on one another. The refined and civilized qualities of the Savage Man are due entirely to his lineage. His growth as a creature of the forest has not prevented the development of humane feelings. As his birthright, he has retained the characteristics of his noble origins. Yet *The Faerie Queene* presents many examples of knights such as Sir Turpine who conduct themselves most ignobly, or who for a time mistake the paths of chivalry. Spenser implies that gentle breeding is in itself neither a guarantee nor a *sine qua non* of virtuous and courtly behavior, even if it is a customary concomitant.[15]

A noble savage found his way onto the stage by the early 1580s when the medieval romance of *Valentine and Orson* had been turned into a long-acted play. Sir Philip Sidney mentions it as an old war-horse in the *Apology for Poetry*. And, interestingly enough, like *Mucedorus*, *Valentine and Orson* continued to be performed for many years by the Queen's Men, a company that flourished in the decade after 1583.[16] The story clearly made for popular theater: it was entered in the Stationers' Register both in 1595 and in 1600. Moreover, in 1598 Henslowe paid Munday and Hathaway five pounds 'for a Booke called Vallentyne & orson.'[17] We will have to reconstruct the essential elements of the fable from sixteenth-century prose versions since no playhouse text has survived.[18] But these efforts will prove rewarding because one of the title characters will serve us well as a prototype for a different kind of savage man.

The story of Valentine and Orson begins with the banishment of the innocent and chaste Queen Bellissant, wife of Alexander, Emperor of Constantinople, and sister of King Pepin of France. Wrongly convinced of her infidelity, Alexander exiles his pregnant wife, who gives birth to twin boys while traveling in a forest outside Orleans. One infant is stolen by a bear, who rears him with her cubs; the other is discovered by King Pepin's men and brought up at court. Years later, the young courtier Valentine undertakes to prove his valor by overpowering a fierce savage man who ravages the forest near Orleans. The struggle between these two powerful and equally matched combatants ends when the wild man surrenders not

---

[15] 'Spenser is not enough of an optimist to espouse the view that the aristocracy possesses out-and-out moral superiority.' Tonkin, p. 162.

[16] *Apology for Poetry* ed. by Geoffrey Shepherd, p. 135. The title page and Stationers' Register information are cited in W. W. Greg, *Elizabethan Stage* IV, pp. 403–404.

[17] *Henslowe's Diary*, edited by R. A. Foakes and R. T. Rickert, p. 93.

[18] The most detailed study of the story will be found in Arthur Dickson, *Valentine and Orson, A Study in Late Medieval Romance*.

to Valentine's superior strength but to his gentle words and to what one version calls the 'force of nature.' The bear-son responds intuitively to feelings, values, and patterns of behavior that are beyond the capacities of the purely bestial. He submits to Valentine and accompanies him to court. Gradually acculturated, Orson protects Valentine in their many adventures. At last, through the aid of tokens and the oracular pronouncements of a brazen head, their true relationship is disclosed. Orson is granted the power of speech – under instruction from the brazen head, a thread under his tongue is cut – their mother is found and exonerated, and the tale ends with the reunion and reconciliation of the family and the marriages of the brothers to Christian princesses.

A child of royal or at least of noble blood who has been raised exclusively by and among animals is not an uncommon inhabitant of a pastoral setting. Such a creature naturally exhibits some of the attributes of the savage man we have discussed earlier: speechlessness, great strength, near nudity, domination over the animal kingdom. But since this particular type is of aristocratic lineage, he is endowed with an innate sensitivity, compassion, and gentility that one does not find among animals.

These qualities of the noble savage are well understood by Shakespeare, for he portrays similar characters in *Cymbeline*. The two brothers in this play are probably the closest parallels in Shakespeare's works to the friendship and rivalry in brotherly love dramatized in *Valentine and Orson*, and Orson's improbable wet nurse and rearing find an approximation in the histories of Cymbeline's sons, Guiderius and Arviragus.

When two and three years old, these princes were kidnapped by the banished general Belarius, who has acted as their father for the last twenty years. Although they have been raised as foresters in a Welsh cave, nevertheless their character has been determined by their blood:

> though train'd up thus meanly,
> I' th' cave wherein they bow, their thoughts do hit
> The roofs of palaces, and Nature prompts them
> In simple and low things to prince it, much
> Beyond the tricks of others. (III.iii.82–86)

And just to ensure that we do not miss the point, we are constantly reminded of it by the moralizing of Belarius:

> 'Tis wonder
> That an invisible instinct should frame them
> To royalty unlearn'd, honour untaught,
> Civility not seen from other, valour
> That wildly grows in them, but yields a crop
> As if it had been sow'd. (IV.ii.176–181)

The elements of the play taken as a whole, however, provide a more coherent action than the earlier version of the story which included near-twins, banishments, slanders, adventures, coincidences, and reconciliations.[19] The nominal hero of this play, Posthumus, is still another son of noble parentage reared parentless. Orphaned at birth, he has been brought up at court like Valentine. There he acquires 'all the learnings that his time/ Could make him the receiver of, which he took,/ As we do air, fast as 'twas minister'd.' Good seeds, it seems, will grow in any soil; Posthumus without family at court or Cymbeline's sons roughing it in the hills of Wales are examples of men with innate virtue.

Cymbeline's step-son Cloten, on the other hand, has nothing to commend him. A fool and a braggart, a gambler on bowls and cards, one who 'Cannot take two from twenty, for his heart,/ And leave eighteen,' is, nevertheless, the child of 'a woman that/ Bears all down with her brain.' The wickedness and scheming of the Queen are reflected in Cloten's plan to revenge himself on Imogen by raping her and killing Posthumus. Cloten is clearly the equal of his mother in his cruel and malicious intentions, but he lacks her cleverness and intelligence. As Imogen is more sensible than her father, so Cloten is less capable than his mother. And in the conflict between step-brothers – a version of the combat between Valentine and Orson – we can rightly anticipate that Guiderius will not reform Cloten but eliminate him.

In *Cymbeline*, we hear the variations played on melodies sounded more simply by the *Valentine and Orson* story. There, we will recall, the resolution was accomplished through the aid of a brazen head; here the final turning point of the action occurs in Posthumus's dream, a dream in which Jupiter on his eagle answers the pleas of Posthumus's family. This dream sequence focuses the action on the fundamental philosophical question at the heart of the matter: the balance of the gifts of Fortune with the gifts of Nature. In Posthumus, according to his father, 'Great nature like his ancestry, moulded the stuff so fair/ That he deserved the praise o' th' world.' Yet this worthy hero is made to suffer an inappropriate fortune: he has never received 'The graces for his merits due.'

Jupiter's answer, illogical but consistent with the hero's career, explains that worthiness and fortune are not in accord: 'Whom best I love I cross; to make my gift,/ The more delay'd, delighted.' The misfortunes of his life, according to Jupiter, ultimately will leave Posthumus 'happier much by his affliction made.' Sorrow will be the cause of joy, misfortune of happiness, and what is long awaited will be all the more pleasurably experienced. Unlike *Valentine and Orson*, in which adventure is the sum and substance, *Cymbeline* provides a rationale for the disparate events of the romance, which proves to be a mode capable of handling more than simply exciting incidents. In its treatment of the materials of romance, in its use of the conventions of the pastoral, and in its skillful combination of diverse thematic and intellectual elements, *Cymbeline* is a play more com-

---

[19] For an analysis of Shakespeare's debt to the romance tradition see E. C. Pettet, *Shakespeare and the Romance Tradition*. Rosalie Colie discusses the pastoral aspect of *Cymbeline* and its treatment of the nature-nurture opposition, p. 242ff.

plicated, more sophisticated, and more philosophical than any pastoral tragicomedy that had preceded it.

The third category of savage man is the most human, the most subtle, complex, and popular. This species is composed of those who reject civilized life, take up residence alone, and gradually reverse the process of acculturation that Orson had undergone. Their reasons for fleeing the society of men may vary, but most frequently they are either ordered into exile or banishment – usually as a result of slander – or they suffer from the betrayal of love or friendship.

In the hands of fine writers, frustration over love and life, tormenting and denigrating, is a subject that can receive sensitive and powerful treatment, for it can transform a cultured individual into a depressed creature, withdrawn and silent. To turn for a last time to *The Fairie Queene*, we notice that Spenser, in relating the tale of Amoret, moves quickly from presenting one type of savage man to another. After the hideous beast of greedie lust has been killed by Belphoebe, she finds her knight Timias offering solace to the terrified and swooning Amoret:

> From her faire eyes wiping the deawy wet,
> Which softly stild, and kissing them atweene,
> And handling soft the hurts, which she did get,
> For of that Carle she sorely bruz'd had beene,
> Als of his own rash hand one wound was to be seene.   (IV.vii.)

Observing Timias's actions 'with sodaine glauncing eye,' Belphoebe, scarcely controlling her urge to punish them both, turns on Timias: 'Is this the faith, she said, and said no more,/ But turnd her face, and fled away for evermore.' Although it can eliminate lust, virginity is nonetheless subject to jealousy. Belphoebe refuses to hear Timias's explanation. Punished by 'her sharpe reproofe,' tormented by the 'dread of her displeasures,' and, finally, left without 'hope of grace,' Timias retreats to the depths of the forest: 'Unto those woods he turned backe againe,/ Full of sad anguish, and in heavy case,' where the 'shade,/ And sad melancholy' can match his mood. There he builds a cabin in a 'gloomy glade,' throws away his weapons, shuns society, redesigns his clothing,

> And his faire lockes, that wont with ointment sweet
> To be embaulm'd, and sweat out dainty dew,
> He let to grow and griesly to concrew,
> Uncomb'd, uncurl'd, and carelessly unshed,
> That in short time his face they overgrew,
> And over all his shoulders did dispred,
> That who he whilome was, uneath was to be red.   (IV.vii.)

Living in isolation and despondency, he is forgotten by his fellow men and so transformed that even Arthur does not recognize his former squire. Language, too, is lost through grief. To Arthur's words, Timias

> aunswered no whit,
> But stood still mute, as if he had beene dum,
> Ne sign of sence did shew, ne common wit,
> As one with grief and anguishe overcum
> And unto every thing did aunswere mum. (IV.vii.)

Unable to rouse him to intelligible response, Arthur leaves the 'strange wight' until 'time for him should remedy provide,/ And him restore to former grace againe.' But the Prince has some notion that the 'rude brutishnesse' of this forest creature conceals a 'gentle swaine,' for he has engraved every tree with 'the name ... Which likly was his liefest love to be,/ For whom he now so sorely was bestad.'

And, in fact, the state of living in the forest or of being out of one's mind has a linguistic basis: according to Bernheimer, wildness and insanity were almost interchangeable terms.[20] Furthermore, a factual basis underlies this confusion: the harmless insane were allowed to wander freely, and they could be taken for wild men.

In describing Timias's anguish, Spenser seems concerned to demonstrate how severely one may suffer in love and how wisdom may be gained in suffering. Later, when he is once again accepted into Belphoebe's favor, Timias seems to comprehend the full joys of his non-physical love for her. He has learned finally to delight in what is the proper relationship between them, and he is no longer troubled by those emotions that had seemed so impossible to control when he had first met her and 'her matchlesse beautie him dismayd.'

Traditional Renaissance sources provided other examples of the civilized man turned savage. The sudden madness that afflicts the proud king Nebuchadnezzar, who 'was driven from men, and did eat grass as oxen, and his body was wet with the dew of heaven, till his hairs were grown like eagles' feathers, and his nails like birds' claws' (Daniel IV.25), is an Old Testament instance of the power of the deity. And Ariosto in the Orlando Furioso describes a hero who demonstrates the power of frustrated love. Distressed to find that Angelica has been untrue, Orlando 'Did on the sudden all his sense enrage/ With hate, with fury, with revenge, and rage' – to quote from Sir John Harrington's translation (1591).[21] After a frenzy of destruction, Orlando collapses into a catatonic state for three days to emerge 'with rage and not with reason waked,/ He rents his clothes and runs about stark naked,' tearing up trees and terrorizing herdsmen and shepherds. When Astolfo finds Orlando some 15 cantos later, we learn 'such a change/ There was in all his shape from top to toe/ He rather seemed a beast more than a man in show.'

Perhaps this also describes how Orlando was performed in the theater, for the stage direction in Robert Greene's Orlando Furioso simply announces: 'enter Orlando attired like a mad-man.' In any case, the presen-

---

[20] P. 12.
[21] Canto 23, p. 185.

tation was a popular one. The play seems to have been in the repertory of
the Queen's Men, the Lord Admiral's, and Lord Strange's, who acted it at
the Rose in 1591/2. Quarto editions appeared in 1594 and again in 1599.

The popularity of this drama is based on the broadest kind of appeal.
The hero suffers no tragic loss of heroic dimension, the action presents no
pathetic contrast between his former glory and his present misery, and the
poetry suggests none of the rich and subtle irony of Ariosto's attitude
toward love.

> But thrice hath Cynthia changde her hiew
> Since thou infected with a lunasie,
> Hast gadded up and downe these lands & groves
> Performing strange and ruthfull stratagems,
> All for the love of faire Angelica,
> Whom thou with Medor didst suppose plaide false,
> But Sacrepant had graven these rundelaies
> To sting thee with infecting jealousie.   (1317–1324)

Here one finds merely spectacle, bombast, and slapstick. Unlike Timias,
Orlando never demonstrates how profound are the consequences of
unrequited love or how passion and grief may lead to patience and
wisdom.

Shakespeare finds this somewhat depressed and misanthropic figure
interesting enough to give us several versions. In Pericles, for example, the
hero displays the characteristics of the wild man. Believing both his wife
and daughter dead, Pericles 'swears/ Never to wash his face, nor cut his
hairs.' And when his ship reaches Mytilene, we are told 'for this three
months [he] hath not spoken/ To any one, nor taken sustenance/ But to
prorogue his grief.'

We can learn, perhaps, even more of the savage appearance of this hero
from the description in George Wilkins's Painfull Adventures of Pericles Prince of
Tyre (1608) – a narrative that combines aspects of Shakespeare's sources
with knowledge of a stage version, quite possibly Shakespeare's own.[22]
According to Wilkins, Pericles in his grief appeared 'attired from the
ordinary habite of other men, as with a long over-growne beard, diffused
hayre, undecent nayles on his fingers, and himselfe lying uppon his
cowch groveling on his face.' When a visitor called his name, 'hee arose up
sodainely with a fierce countenaunce: but seeing him to be a stranger,
verie comely and honourably attyred, hee shruncke himselfe downe
uppon his pillow, and held him peace.' When Marina comes to console

---

[22] F. D. Hoeniger and Thomas Edwards argue in 'An Approach to the Problem of Pericles,'
Shakespeare Survey V (1952), 25–49 that the novel was affected by Shakespeare's dramatization.
Kenneth Muir in Shakespeare as Collaborator (New York, 1960) and Gerald Barker, 'Themes and
Variations in Shakespeare's Pericles,' English Studies, (1963), 44:401–444, claim rather that
Wilkins was a source for Shakespeare's play. I have used Geoffrey Bullough, Narrative and
Dramatic Sources VI, p. 541, for my citations from Wilkins.

him, she finds a man even more violent than his counterpart in the play, for Wilkins explains that 'in his rash distemperature' Pericles does not merely push the young woman away but strikes her so powerfully on the face that she falls into a swoon, bleeding.

Shakespeare's Pericles, having found incest, fraud, and jealousy among men, having felt the loss of all he held dear, and having seen nature seemingly indifferent both to human injustice and human misery, becomes something less than human in his catatonia.

Perhaps we are being made the witnesses of his profound suffering in order that we can wonder and delight in his change of fortune. In his reunion with Marina, sorrow and happiness seem to meet; opposing and intense emotions are juxtaposed so that we can watch the merging "Twixt two extremes of passion, joy and grief,' as Edgar describes his reconciliation with his own father. But unlike the deaths in King Lear, the destinies of parents in this play are more fortunate, even though the gods remain as ambiguous. Pericles tells Marina: 'O, I am mock'd,/ And thou by some incensed god sent hither/ To make the world to laugh at me.'

The course of the action traces Pericles' pain so that we, too, might share in the 'great sea of joys' that now overwhelms him with its sweetness and makes 'past miseries sport.' This commixture of contradictory emotions, the merging of irreconcilable opposites in the story itself, expresses something fundamental to the meaning of the play and basic to its presentation. The conventions of the savage man have been used to dramatize how sorrow may lead a strong man to reject his own humanity, how a hero may imitate the beast in his desire to escape the shocks that flesh is heir to. But such efforts can never succeed fully, for what is inhuman is not only incapable of man's anguish but also ignorant of his bliss. The intensity of his final happiness is the measure of Pericles' former sorrows just as the recovery of his daughter marks the rebirth of her father to his true humanity: 'Thou that beget'st him that did thee beget.' And when he cries out ecstatically, 'Give me my robes; I am wild in my beholding,' his desire to change garments marks his return to normalcy, for this 'wildness' is the elation and excitement of a rational mind.

The references to King Lear in the discussion of Pericles point up how closely related this tragedy is to the romances that followed it; indeed, to paraphrase Goneril, the observation so many have made of this hath not been little. Moreover, we can hardly fail to notice that Edgar embodies many of the characteristics we have identified as belonging to the savage man.

In a work that asks what essential differences separate the human and the animal world, we should not be surprised to find Edgar portrayed as a type of savage man. He tells us himself that in his disguise as Poor Tom he will mortify his flesh, 'elf' all his hair in knots, grime his face with filth, and take 'the basest and most poorest shape/ That ever penury, in contempt of man,/ Brought near to beast.' Since the appearance of the Bedlam beggar has an historical reality, we must allow a degree of realism to his words. Nevertheless, what Edgar dramatizes in his disguise is a vision of 'man/

Brought near to beast.' And that is an appropriate sight in a play full of animal imagery and crowded with comparisons of man to animal: daughters are 'dog-hearted'; bears are tied by the neck, men by the legs; women are as lascivious as the fitchew and the soiled horse; on a night when 'The lion and the belly-pinched wolf/ Keep their fur dry,' King Lear unbonneted runs onto the stormy heath.

With the sight of Poor Tom, naked and shivering, Lear truly understands that 'unaccommodated man is no more but such a poor, bare, forked animal.' He had only moments before come to the realization that man stripped of those comforts that reinforce his human identity is simply another creature without distinction or importance. Now, in his encounter with Poor Tom, Lear reaches a new awareness. Reducing human existence to its essentials debases it: 'Man's life is cheap as beast's.' If man is more than or inherently different from the animal, the distinctions must rest not with physical or material qualities, but with rational and spiritual values, with notions of duty, ceremonious affection, kindness, pity, fortitude, and forgiveness.

Moreover, as Poor Tom, Edgar takes on all the evils that flesh is capable of: the cruelty and lust of Goneril and Regan, the calculated self-interest of Edmund, the self-serving immorality of Oswald.

> A serving man, proud in heart and mind . . . . [One that] swore as many oaths as I spake words, and broke them in the sweet face of heaven; one that slept in the contriving of lust. . . . False of heart, light of ear, bloody of hand; hog in sloth, fox in stealth, wolf in greediness, dog in madness, lion in prey.
>
> (III.iv.85–95)

And in the same way Edgar shares in the lives of the good characters, knowing like the Fool, Kent, and Cordelia what it is to be 'whipp'd from tithing to tithing, and stocked, punish'd, and imprison'd.' In the words of one of Beckett's tramps, 'He's all humanity.'

In enacting the role of Poor Tom, Edgar embodies the lowest pitch of human existence – Gloucester recalls that the sight of the beggar made him think a man a worm. But through Edgar's various impersonations we watch him reestablish order and hierarchy among humanity. Starting with the bare, forked animal, 'the thing itself,' Edgar becomes by turns peasant, soldier, knight incognito, and perhaps even king.[23] He stands for the great range of human potential in behavior and class at the same time that he reminds us of the 'narrow distance between nobleman and beggar, accomodated man and the forked animal.' Through his variety of disguises he portrays not only man's closeness to the beast but also his distance from the animal. And in emphasizing man's common humanity, Edgar is perhaps the most powerful, poignant, and comprehensive presentation of the savage man in literature.

---

[23] Bernard McElroy, *Shakespeare's Mature Tragedies*, p. 159.

Whether presented as sub-human, as a man reared in a state of nature, or as a man who has rejected the society of his fellows, embodiments of the savage man seem to pervade Renaissance literature. His frequent appearances are understandable, for he is a popular type character with audiences and writers. The wild man can have an immediate and powerful effect on his audience at the same time as he can contain and express a wide range of meanings for an author. In his antics, the savage man could delight and terrify, and his behavior could demonstrate that life in a state of nature is possibly inferior – or possibly superior – to 'civilized' life. Furthermore, the savage man's removal from society allowed him to display the effects of heredity and environment on individual development. Finally, the wild man represented an important link in that chain which, by degrees, connects everything in creation. And while he provides the bridge between the human and the animal, he also clarifies the distinctions beween man and beast.

That this literary creation can do so much so well explains his durability, for the wild man has managed to keep his hold on the imagination of civilized man despite the encroachments of science and technology. His progeny occasionally appeared in the antimasques of the Jacobean court, where their savage behavior set off the harmony and beauty of the proceedings. Later writers as diverse as Swift and Rousseau, philosophers as opposed as Hobbes and Locke have also appreciated the symbolic value of this creation. If Bremo, or Orson, or Orlando are not familiar names today, modern readers may recognize their offspring more readily in such nineteenth and twentieth century characters as Mowgli, or Tarzan, or King Kong.

IV

The Overreacher

In Renaissance drama, the overreacher, like the savage man, represents an extreme of human nature. But in contrast to the savage who demonstrates humanity at its basest, the overreacher reveals mankind at the height of its potential, achieving superhuman mastery of space, time, power, or knowledge. Since such figures can command the stage by their energy and ability, often generating the action of the entire plot through the forcefulness of their nature, they are both popular and useful characters for a playwright. In addition, they appealed to the Renaissance interest in the 'singular' individual that Burckhardt considered one of the distinguishing marks of this period. And, of course, these dynamic, able, and often charismatic figures helped prove the theory advanced by Renaissance historiographers that the course of history is shaped more by men than by Providence. The great variety of overreachers who hold major roles in Renaissance English drama and the strikingly different attitudes of Elizabethan and Jacobean playwrights toward this character are vividly demonstrated in Marlowe's *Tamburlaine Parts I and II* (1587/1588) and *Doctor Faustus* (1592), Jonson's *The Alchemist* (1610), Shakespeare's *The Tempest* (1611), and Massinger's *A New Way To Pay Old Debts* (1625).

The essential qualities that identify an overreacher are easily recognized.[1] Above all, he must demonstrate that widely admired Renaissance trait of *virtú*, a combination of dazzling strength and energy, which is used in the service of self-advancement. Satisfaction of the will is the aim of the overreacher, and all his efforts are directed to this end. So intense is his ambition and so forceful is his character that he persists, striving against all odds, on a course in which only the extraordinary man can succeed. Moreover, he works directly and openly. The overreacher acts with astonishing candor, announcing his intentions and his means. His behavior is not marked by the trickery or guile characteristic of a

---

[1] The most thorough study of the overreacher's classical ancestry and his characteristics in Renaissance drama will be found in Eugene Waith's *The Herculean Hero in Marlowe, Chapman, Shakespeare, and Dryden*.

Machiavel.[2] He reveals openly, without deviousness or fraud, the power and cleverness of the lion and the fox recommended by Machiavelli.

Such a character arrived on the Elizabethan stage by a complicated process. A portion of its ancestry is Biblical and first appeared in medieval drama, for some elements can be found in the raging Herod of the Coventry cycle:

> ...the whole Orent ys under myn obbeydeance,
> And Prynce am I of Purgatorre, and Cheff
>   Capten of Hell!
> And those tyraneos trayturs be force ma I compell
> Myne enmyis to vanquese, and evyn to dust them dryve,
> And with a twynke of myn iee not won to be lafte alyve.[3]
>
> (502–506)

The overreacher's character also owes something to the quasi-historical drama of the early Elizabethan stage. Thomas Preston's *Cambyses, King of Persia* (1561), for example, has for its title character a king who defies all restraints:

> Who dare say nay what I pretend, who dare the same withstand
> Shall lose his head, and have report as traitor through my land.
> There is no nay.   (79–81)

But such figures as Herod and King Cambises, despite their tyrannical power and egotism, are only forerunners. They lack the enthusiasm for conquest, the imaginative scope and infinite aspiration, that mark the true overreacher.

The heroic, near-divine qualities of the overreacher evolved not exclusively within England but also from classical examples which were grafted onto native stock. Mythological precedents are numerous: Marlowe compares Tamburlaine to Zeus, who rebelled against his father to become king of the gods; and he compares Faustus both to Icarus, who dared to fly too high, and to Phaeton, who tried to drive Apollo's chariot across the heavens. Shakespeare gives Prospero in *The Tempest* god-like powers over nature: the great duke has even 'rifted Jove's stout oak/ With his own bolt.' And both Sir Epicure Mammon in *The Alchemist* and Sir Giles Overreach in *A New Way To Pay Old Debts* compare themselves with Hercules. In fact, Hercules, the son of Zeus and Alcmena, part god and part man, is a favorite model, embodying many of the overreacher's qualities: absolute fidelity to his own principles of behavior; the ability to perform great feats of courage and strength; the capacity to love; sensitivity to beauty; savage anger; and, finally, the stoicism to endure pain, madness, and death.

---

[2] This forthrightness is typical of the purest examples of the overreacher. Characters such as Marlowe's Barabas or Jonson's Sejanus are hybrids, demonstrating something of the overreacher's ambition and energy which have been joined to a talent for Machiavellian scheming.

[3] Adams, *Pre-Shakespearean Drama*, p. 159.

By the last quarter of the century, the combined effects of the educational system and the availability of translations of Greek and Latin literature greatly increased the influence of classical writing – for example, Seneca's treatment of the Hercules story in *Hercules Furens* first appeared in English in 1561. But the adoption of these mythological figures as prototypes for the overreacher was not simply a consequence of their imaginative appeal for English writers of the late sixteenth and early seventeenth century. The general literary climate was made ripe for such a grandiose figure in part through the influence of the religious controversy of the time.

Indeed, the interpretation of the overreacher that the playwrights of this period presented was profoundly affected by some of the prevailing religious ideas. For example, the powerful language, strong images, and sweeping climaxes of their ringing phrases suggest that these overreachers were expressing what in Calvinist theology was the certainty of one's own salvation, a zealous and bold affirmation of one's place among the Elect. According to Calvinist teaching, neither deeds nor conduct were reliable indicators of personal redemption, but one's own assurance 'became the sign of salvation, a sign which only the believer himself could recognize.'[4] Calvin insists that the true believer 'leaning upon the assurance of his salvation, confidently triumphs over the devil and death.'[5] This confidence based on faith enabled Puritan preachers to employ a 'rhetoric of assurance' in their sermons, 'to proclaim their uprightness without seeming to boast or succumb to self-admiration, and to encourage their audiences to feel the confidence which would signify their election.'[6] And so some of the overreacher's vaunting language may well derive its tone from imitating the assured speech of those who confidently proclaim themselves among the Elect.

Although some Calvinists might announce the certainty of their own salvation, all Elizabethans, Calvinists and non-Calvinists alike, must have experienced deep feelings of doubt and anxiety, if not from spiritual considerations than from political ones. Only in the last quarter of the century did England, exhausted, settle its religious controversy by accepting the Elizabethan compromise, for the country had changed its official religion three times in the preceding twenty-five years. During such a time of change, all religious views were open to charges of heresy. Those who accepted Rome's authority as well as those who questioned it had been subjected to an official process of rejection and readoption – Catholic martyrs executed on Tower Hill after Henry VIII's break with Rome were replaced by Protestant martyrs burned at Smithfield when Henry's older daughter Mary became Queen. Even the most fanatical would have been aware that other conceptions of man's nature than their own and other

---

[4] Martha Tuck Rozett, *The Doctrine of Election and the Emergence of Elizabethan Tragedy*, p. 43.

[5] *Institutes*, translated by F. L. Battles, edited by John T. McNeil, Vols. XX, 557ff.; XXI, 784.

[6] Rozett, p. 49.

definitions of the good life, however mistaken, had devoted adherents. And all Englishmen recognized that by marriage or death, Elizabeth could again change everything. Every opinion about man's inherent character or goals had been affirmed, denied, and reaffirmed while every believer feared that his own faith could once again be challenged or outlawed. Since sharply differing views of humanity, of man's potential for growth or change, are expressed in the teachings of Catholicism and the various branches of Protestantism, we should not be surprised by the range and variety of points of view reflected in the dramas of Marlowe, Jonson, Shakespeare, and their contemporaries.

Before considering the treatment of the overreacher by these playwrights, we should become aware of the variety of conceptions of man's capabilities held at this time. Surely the most idealistic and extreme interpretation of man's proper pursuit was argued by the Florentine Neoplatonist Pico della Mirandola (1463–1494), who believed that man's possibilities are limitless since he is 'the only creature whose life is determined not by nature but by his own free choice.' In his influential Oration, probably written in 1486 but printed only after his death, Pico claimed man was the last of God's creations in the universe, but the one with the greatest potential:

When the work was finished, the Craftsman kept wishing that there was someone to ponder the plan of so great a work, to love its beauty, and to wonder at its vastness. Therefore, when everything was done . . ., he finally took thought concerning the creation of man. But there was not among His archetypes that from which He could fashion a new offspring, nor was there in His treasurehouses anything which He might bestow on His new son as an inheritance. . . . All was now complete; all things had been assigned to the highest, the middle, and the lowest orders. But in its final creation it was not the part of the Father's powers to fail as though exhausted. . . .
At last the best of artisans ordained that that creature to whom He had been able to give nothing proper to himself should have joint possession of whatever had been peculiar to each of the different kinds of being. He therefore took man as a creature of indeterminate nature and, assigning him a place in the middle of the world, addressed him thus: 'Neither a fixed abode nor a form that is thine alone nor any function peculiar to thyself have we given thee, Adam. . . . The nature of all other beings is limited and constrained within the bounds of laws prescribed by us. Thou, constrained by no limits, in accordance with thine own free will, in whose hand We have set thee at the world's center that thou mayest from thence more easily observe whatever is in the world. We have made thee neither of heaven nor of earth, neither mortal nor immortal, so that with freedom of choice and with honor, as though maker and molder thyself, thou mayest fashion thyself in whatever shape thou shalt prefer. Thou shalt have the power to degenerate. . . . Thou shalt have the power, out of thy soul's judgment, to be reborn into the higher forms, which are divine.'[7]

---

[7] Translated by Elizabeth Livermore Forbes in The Renaissance Philosophy of Man, edited by Ernest Cassirer, Paul Oskar Kristeller, and John Randall, Jr., pp. 224–225.

Pico then draws an extraordinary conclusion from his extraordinary fable: Adam is told that he may 'possess what abode, what form, and what functions thou thyself shalt desire.' Since human beings are totally free, they should use this freedom, driven by a 'holy ambition,' to 'pant after the highest and ... toil with all our strength to obtain it.' Indeed, Pico goes on to say that human beings should challenge the angels and 'intolerant of a lower place, emulate their dignity and their glory. If we have willed it, we shall be second to them in nothing.'[8] In other words, all man's efforts should be applied to attaining what is finest and noblest. Pico influenced the characterization of the overreacher by glorifying man's potential and his boundless aspirations, even though Pico's noble idealism was frequently ignored.

Pico's ideas and the influence of the Florentine Academy to which he belonged reached England early in the sixteenth century. John Colet, Dean of St Paul's, founder of St Paul's school and spiritual mentor to Thomas More, was in correspondence with Marsilio Ficino, who was appointed by Cosimo de' Medici to preside over the Neoplatonist school, and Sir Thomas More himself translated Pico's biography and some of his letters. Certainly, Pico's ideals were widely known and discussed in intellectual circles as his writings or others inspired by them circulated among the educated. Readers later in the century could also find Montaigne writing in a similar vein when he describes the restless mind and discontented spirit as characteristics of the superior individual:

> It is a sign of failing powers or of weariness when the mind is content. No generous spirit stays within itself; it constantly aspires and rises above its own strength. It leaps beyond its attainments. If it does not advance, and push forward, if it does not strengthen itself, and struggle with itself, it is only half alive. Its pursuits have no bounds or rules; its food is wonder, search, and ambiguity.[9]

But Pico and Montaigne's were not the only or even the most widespread conceptions among the English. And although their view of humanity extols human potentialities, some Protestants, more influential still in England, promulgated a very different notion of man's basic nature. The Calvinist view of man, in fact, was fundamentally different – one is born either saved or damned. If saved, then one can confidently proclaim one's greatness. If, on the other hand, one lacks this self-assurance, one may well be among the more numerous corrupt who are irrevocably predestined for damnation. In any case, man cannot achieve freedom through the exercise of his will or his reason. Naturally, such a view is hardly congenial to the overreacher's character. According to Luther:

> Free choice can belong to the majesty of God alone, because it is his power which makes and wills everything in the sky and on the earth. If one at-

---

[8] P. 227.
[9] The Third Book of Essais, 1588, translated by J. M. Cohen. Quoted in Rozett, p. 166.

tributes it to man one attributes to him nothing less than divinity itself; but there can be no greater sacrilege.[10]

Protestants could be as extreme and persuasive in the expression of their beliefs as Pico. Although he demonstrates more of a rhetorical flourish, Calvin restates Luther's position in as firm and absolute a manner:

> We are not our own; therefore, neither is our own reason or will to rule our acts and counsels. We are not our own; therefore, let us not make it our end to seek what may be agreeable to our carnal nature. We are not our own; therefore, as far as possible, let us forget ourselves and the things that are ours. On the other hand, we are God's; let us, therefore, live and die to him.[11]

In contrast to their brand of Protestantism, a more moderate position was proposed by Richard Hooker, the official apologist for the Anglican Church. Nevertheless, Hooker's reasoning leaves him far closer to the conservatism of Luther and Calvin than to the liberalism of Pico. In *Of the Laws of Ecclesiastical Polity*, Hooker argues that natural law was established when God commanded 'those things to be which are, and to be in such sort as they are, to keep that tenure and course which they do.' Since that time:

> heaven and earth have hearkened unto his voice, and their labour hath been to do his will. ... Now if nature should intermit her course, and leave altogether though it were but for a while the observation of her own laws; if the moon should wander from her beaten way, the times and seasons of the year blend themselves by disordered and confused mixture, the winds breathe out their last gasp, the clouds yield no rain, the earth be defeated of heavenly influence, the fruits of the earth pine away as children at the withered breasts of their mother no longer able to yield them relief: what would become of man himself, whom these things now do all serve? See we not plainly that obedience of creatures unto the law of nature is the stay of the whole world?[12]

All depends, here, on man's obedience to God's law and on man's acceptance of his fixed position in the overall scheme of things. Since such a strictly ordered universe does not permit man to rise from his place, the overreacher's ambition runs counter to divine law and his desires are disruptive of universal peace.

Yet Hooker, though influential and highly admired, was not perhaps the ideal spokesman for Elizabethan Protestantism, for he may not have expressed the central, or most popularly held opinions.[13] Several widely followed preachers, such as the staunch William Perkins, were even more

---

[10] Quoted by Leontine Zanta, *La Renaissance du Stoicisme au XVIeme Siècle* (Paris, 1914), and translated by Hiram Haydn in *The Counter-Renaissance*.

[11] *Institutes*, III.vii.1, translated by Henry Beveridge, as quoted in Alan Sinfield, *Literature in Protestant England 1550–1660*, p. 84.

[12] Book I, III.2. pp. 156–157.

[13] According to Sinfield, 'The centrality in Elizabethan thought which modern Anglicans have accorded to Hooker's words is quite unjustified.' p. 14.

outspoken in their warnings about man's ambitions. For example, Perkins fiercely condemns the quality of magnificence or magnanimity, a virtue derived from Aristotle's *Nichomachean Ethics*, that both Sidney in *The Defense of Poetry* and Spenser in the *Letter to Raleigh* consider the cardinal virtue necessary for a man to attain the perfect heroic life.[14] Perkins even denies that it is a virtue at all:

> the scope and the end of this virtue (as they term it) is to make men to attempt high and great matters above their reach, and so to go beyond their callings. Besides, it is directly opposite to the virtue of humility, which teacheth that a man ought always to be base, vile, and lowly in his own eyes.[15]

Perkins' more limited, narrow, and stern view of human potential is probably closer to the mainstream of Elizabethan thought at the turn of the century than is Hooker's more kindly and lyrical opinion. Indeed, from 1591–1600, Perkins's *Golden Chain* was reprinted twelve times.

When such writers as Marlowe, Jonson, Shakespeare, and Massinger turn their hands to creating overreachers – larger-than-life individuals – their versions reflect not only the set qualities of this stereotype but also the broad range of interpretations of man's nature and capabilities that, as we have seen, were a consequence of the new learning and of the continuing religious controversy. For example, the extreme self-assurance of the presumptuous hero was ambiguous. Protestantism condemned his attitude, but at the same time it argued that the vaunting, boastful language of the overreacher might just be, after all, expressing his manifest certainty that he is indeed one of the Elect, confident of his own salvation.

Marlowe's *Tamburlaine* has as its hero a paradigm of the overreacher who has attained supreme physical strength and worldly power.[16] Even his godlike appearance – tall, muscular, stern, blond, and handsome – reinforces his assertion that he can accomplish whatever he sets out to do. Two of these character traits, extreme pride and self-confidence, are evident from his very first appearance. Although dressed as a rustic, he is no mere country ruffian. The riches he has taken from the beautiful Zenocrate and her train 'Shall be reserved,' and she will be more honored as Tamburlaine's captive, he tells her, 'Than if you were arrived .../ Even in the circle of your father's arms.' Tamburlaine boasts that he is greater than the Cham, the Tartar emperor, and, though born the son of Scythian shepherds, he plans to conquer all Asia and prove 'to be a terror to the world.'

[14] Book IV.3.
[15] Sinfield, p. 37.
[16] In addition to Eugene Waith's work, I am indebted to several studies of Marlowe and to editors of the plays discussed here, especially John Bakeless, Paul Kocher, Harry Levin, Clifford Leech, M. M. Mahood, Irving Ribner, and J. B. Steane.

In a dramatic gesture, he then strips off his shepherd's clothes, 'weeds that I disdain to wear,' and reveals himself glittering in armor. Now Tamburlaine's impressive appearance matches his words, and these are given a kind of confirmation by his followers:

> Methinks I see kings kneeling at his feet,
> And he with frowning brows and fiery looks
> Spurning their crowns from off their captive heads.   (I.ii.55–57)

Zenocrate points out that the gods, who defend the innocent, will oppose Tamburlaine if he keeps her prisoner. But her argument hardly persuades him, for he believes that the gods are his supporters. Indeed, when they later seem to turn against him, Tamburlaine threatens to make war against heaven itself.[17]

Although filled with conceit and arrogance, Marlowe's overreacher is also susceptible to beauty. He offers a series of extreme comparisons as proof of Zenocrate's superiority: 'lovelier,' 'Brighter,' 'fairer,' 'more worth,' 'More rich and valurous.' And as conclusive evidence of her attractiveness, Tamburlaine announces his own love for her.[18] Since he is concerned basically with property and wealth, his values are defined by physical possession – even Zenocrate seems to be an object that Tamburlaine owns. For such a hero, the goods of this world are, naturally, highly prized; Tamburlaine is thrilled by 'golden mines,' 'precious stones,' and an 'imperial crown.'

In the closing episode of the first act, which dramatizes Tamburlaine's encounter with Theridamas, the leader of a thousand Persian horsemen, the overreacher demonstrates his persuasiveness and explains the basis for his self-assurance:

> Forsake thy king and do but join with me,
> And we will triumph over all the world.
> I hold the Fates bound fast in iron chains,
> And with my hand turn Fortune's wheel about
> And sooner shall the sun fall from his sphere
> Than Tamburlaine be slain or overcome.
> Draw forth thy sword, thou mighty man-at-arms,
> Intending but to raze my charmed skin,
> And Jove himself will stretch his hand from heaven
> To ward the blow and shield me safe from harm.   (I.ii. 171–180)

Tamburlaine's claims to superhuman ability and to divine protection are aspects of the overreacher's belief in individual liberty. He seems, in fact, to be adapting Pico's idealistic view of man's potential in his glorification of man as a demigod with absolute freedom of action; Tamburlaine im-

---

[17] Waith suggests that Tamburlaine's 'facile references to the gods, sometimes friendly, sometimes hostile, may be interpreted as part of the heroic character of which Hercules is the prototype.' p. 84.

[18] 'The inclusion in his nature of the capacity to love is a characteristic Renaissance addition to the classical model of the Herculean hero.' Waith, p. 72.

plicitly rejects Luther's argument that free choice belongs to God alone. According to Tamburlaine, mankind can achieve all he desires because his will is free and because his position is not fixed, his place in society is not determined by birth or convention. The cowardly and weak Mycetes, King of Persia, is proof that primogeniture offers a questionable basis for choosing a ruler.

Tamburlaine's words also disagree sharply with the position expressed by Hooker, who argues that mankind can prosper only by following the constant 'tenure and course' of nature. Instead of accepting the Anglican view, the Scythian rebel claims that he follows the precedent of Jove, 'the eldest son of heavenly Ops/ Who thrust his doting father from his chair.' Restless ambition, insatiable aspiration for ever grander and greater accomplishments is, according to Tamburlaine, an innate quality of man in general – and overreachers in particular. The four elements of earth, air, fire, and water are 'Warring within our breasts' and their strife 'Doth teach us all to have aspiring minds'; 'to wear ourselves and never rest' in an unending struggle for self-fullfilment.

Two distinctive aspects of this overreacher are clearly demonstrated in the course of this self-fulfillment. The first is his honesty. All his actions are performed in a direct and open manner. Rather than take the crown privately from the foolish King Mycetes, who is attempting to hide it, Tamburlaine will seize Mycetes's crown in battle. 'I lend it thee,/ 'Till I may see thee hemmed with armed men/ Then shalt thou see me pull it from thy head.' Again, when Tamburlaine decides to oppose Cosroe, whom he has just supported, the Scythian clearly announces his intention:

> Techelles, take a thousand horse with thee,
> And bid him turn him back to war with us,
> That only made him king to make us sport.
> We will not steal upon him cowardly,
> But give him warning and more warriors.　　　　(II.v.99–103)

Nothing underhanded or Machiavellian mars the candor of his behavior. In part, the overreacher is so confident of his success that he does not need to resort to trickery; in part, the overreacher is so naive a hero that deviousness would be out of character.

The second characteristic personality trait of this overreacher is his implacability.

> Tam.　And when they see me march in black array,
> 　　　With mournful streamers hanging down their heads,
> 　　　Were in that city all the world contained,
> 　　　Not one should 'scape, but perish by our swords.
> Zen.　Yet would you have some pity for my sake,
> 　　　Because it is my country's and my father's.
> Tam.　Not for the world, Zenocrate, if I have sworn.
>
> 　　　　　　　　　　　　　　　　　　　　　(IV.ii.119–124)

Once set on a course of action, Tamburlaine is unable to modify his plans without in some way undercutting his own authority. Compromise is unthinkable. By denying the requests of the Virgins of Damascus to spare their city and by refusing Zenocrate's plea to 'take a friendly truce' with the inhabitants, Tamburlaine proves his strength of character. This ability to remain firm, unmoved by considerations of pity or mercy, is further evidence of Tamburlaine's heroic individualism, his determination to satisfy himself alone. The more unyielding Tamburlaine is in holding to his own course of action, no matter how cruel or unreasonable, the greater is the proof of his stature as a hero. 'My customs are as preemptory/ As wrathful planets,' he warns, and his disposition is well known: 'His resolution far exceedeth all.' To some extent, this explains the harshness and brutality of Tamburlaine's reprisals. His heroic temperament, expressed through 'fierie looks' and 'frowning wrath,' may threaten and command but cannot overlook or forgive. When his words are disobeyed, his response cannot be lenient or compassionate, for he must act in ways that prove his inexorable and irresistible will. With his restless energy, this overreacher seems to drive himself even as much as he drives all before him.

Although Part I ends as Tamburlaine 'takes truce with all the world' and weds Zenocrate, one cannot imagine him retiring from the battlefield permanently. Only the most active life could suit so restless a disposition, and only death itself could end it. Appropriately, then, Tamburlaine Part II dramatizes the inevitability and unalterable finality of death, and the fact that the overreacher cannot forever pursue worldly or even other-worldly power. 'Nothing prevails,' Theridamas reminds Tamburlaine, who is 'Raving, impatient, desperate, and mad' over the death of Zenocrate. Tamburlaine, who brings death and destruction to others, must himself experience loss. But in time he naturally turns from mourning Zenocrate to consoling himself by total involvement in the pursuit of military victories:

> I will, with engines never exercised,
> Conquer, sack, and utterly consume
> Your cities and your golden palaces,
> . . .
> And, till by vision or by speech I hear
> Immortal Jove say 'Cease, my Tamburlaine,'
> I will persist a terror to the world.   (IV.i.192–201)

At last, he, too, must confront the 'ugly monster Death.' Tamburlaine, who could never be overcome by any external opponent, is to be defeated from within. The hero first attempts to resist – 'take your swords,/ And threaten him whose hand afflicts my soul' – but he comes to recognize the impossibility of escape – Death 'flies away at every glance I give,/ And when I look away, comes stealing on.' Tamburlaine realizes that he must complete his conquest of the world through the deeds of his sons:

> Give me a map; then let me see how much
> Is left for me to conquer all the world,
> That these, my boys, may finish all my wants.   (V.iii.123–125)

And he comes to endorse as his parting wisdom the greatness of spirit that can accept the inevitable with dignity:

> Let not thy love exceed thine honour, son,
> Nor bar thy mind that magnanimity
> That nobly must admit necessity. (V.iii.199–201)

Tamburlaine encourages his sons to cultivate that Aristotelian magnanimity William Perkins thought so dangerous and questionable a virtue.

Death is terrible for the Marlovian overreacher because it is inexorable and absolute. It is the ultimate denial of the total freedom Tamburlaine has claimed for himself. Tamburlaine has been free to satisfy himself during his life; but, as the sequel teaches, life itself will have an end, and even the drive and energy of the overreacher must have a stop.[19]

Through their action, the *Tamburlaine* plays establish for Renaissance drama the type of the overreacher who gains political power through military conquest. In *Part I* the hero's skill and courage are demonstrated on the battlefield when, outnumbered by more and more opponents, he wins victory after victory. That these victories, which represent man's hold over the goods of this world, cannot be permanent becomes the essential tragic truth for him in *Part II*, an inescapable fact of the human condition.

The compulsion to excel, the drive to exceed the normal or the unusual, can be exercised in realms of human endeavor other than military conquest. *Tamburlaine* explores the paradox of the desire to acquire what cannot ultimately be retained: *Doctor Faustus* considers the human longing for more than mortal knowledge, the paradox of frail and weak man striving to become a god: 'Here try thy brains to get a deity.'

This hero's character is also in many ways typical of the overreacher. He possesses something of the pride and even arrogant self-confidence found in Tamburlaine as well as Tamburlaine's susceptibility to beauty. In addition to his desire for knowledge, Faustus expresses a Tamburlaine-like longing for Indian gold, oriental pearl, the world's 'pleasant fruits and princely delicates.' And like Tamburlaine, Faustus voices aspirations that drive him to the very limits of human potential:

> All things that move between the quiet poles
> Shall be at my command. Emperors and kings
> Are but obeyed in their several provinces,

---

[19] M. M. Mahood in *Poetry and Humanism* observes that '*Tamburlaine the Great* is the only drama I know in which the *death* of the hero constitutes the tragedy. ... Tamburlaine's voyage of self-discovery takes him as far as death before he finds the limits set to his ambition.' p. 60.

> Nor can they raise the wind or rend the clouds,
> But his dominion that exceeds in this
> Stretcheth as far as doth the mind of man.
> A sound magician is a demi-god.   (Sc. 1.57–63)

'A sound magician' is Faustus's chosen career, the means that will enable him to overcome human limitations and live up to Pico's idea of limitless self-fulfillment. He rejects the more socially acceptable vocations – philosopher, doctor, lawyer – because they seem petty; medicine, for example, cannot revive the dead. Faustus also rejects the study of divinity, traditionally considered the highest of all earthly pursuits, as 'Unpleasant, harsh, contemptible and vile.' Christianity, as expounded by St John, he finds particularly demeaning and fatalistic. According to St John, man is a sinful creature, the reward of sin is death, 'And so consequently ... we must die an everlasting death.' These doctrines, which stress Calvinistic notions of original sin and predestination, are repugnant to Faustus because they deny absolute free will and free choice. Nor will Faustus consider how such matters as faith, repentance, the sacrifice of Christ, or the mercy of a forgiving God can alter the 'everlasting death' by a life hereafter. His is a God of denial who forbids and restricts, threatening 'heavy wrath.'

So thoroughly committed is Faustus to his own pursuits that he actually refuses to admit anything that runs counter to his will. He insists on holding to his own view of things even when the evidence proves otherwise. For example, Faustus denies Christian notions of damnation even though Mephistophilis says that he fell with Lucifer and that he carries his own torment within himself. Unlike the central character of a morality play, who may be misled from the path of virtue by the enticements of sin, this hero consciously chooses his course of action. Indeed, he damns himself despite the extraordinary warnings of Mephistophilis: 'O Faustus, leaves these frivolous demands/ Which strike a terror to my fainting soul.'

Still, despite the blindness to anything that contradicts his view of life, Faustus is more sensitive and introspective than Tamburlaine. As an overreacher, he demonstrates a greater self-awareness than the earlier hero. The learned doctor fully realizes that he acts simply to please himself; self-satisfaction is his only motivation. Indeed, his pride and willfulness are so strong that on the one hand, Faustus feels his sin too great even for God to forgive and on the other hand, he feels the requirement that he repent and ask forgiveness to be demeaning. To demand that he conform, to insist that he seek God's love and believe that he can be absolved, is too humbling for one with Faustus's ego. He rejects the love of God in order to serve his own appetite, and he claims that rejecting God's love is a demonstration of his heroism. And yet, one might well argue that it is not Faustus who rejects God, but God who rejects Faustus. According to Calvin, God 'does not allow Satan to have dominion over the souls of believers, but only gives over to his sway the impious and unbelieving, whom he deigns not to number among his flock.' As Alan Sinfield has observed, 'In this view Faustus is not damned because he makes a pact with the Devil, he makes a pact with the Devil because he is damned.'[20]

After signing the agreement with Lucifer, Faustus never again expresses the kind of easy confidence of his earlier uncommitted self, or sounds that note of total mastery struck by Tamburlaine. For his part, the shepherd-warrior is untroubled by questions of morality, for he truly believes a special law applies to him alone. Right and wrong are determined simply by whether they suit Tamburlaine. But Faustus, among the most intelligent and sensitive of overreachers, is far more complex and modern a hero – curious and willful, angst-ridden and tormented, doubting, despairing, and ultimately damned.

For Faustus, torn between conflicting desires, is indeed filled with anguish and inner doubt. Feelings of uncertainty are revived with every offer of divine love and forgiveness – offers that are repeated throughout the play. Early in the action Faustus expresses the assurance of a brash adolescent; for example, he tells Mephistophilis: 'Learn thou of Faustus manly fortitude,/ And scorn those joys thou never shalt possess.' But at most other times, depressed and suicidal, he voices his profound regret over the decision he has made:

> O, would I had never seen Wittenberg, never read book.
> And what wonders I have done, all Germany can witness –
> yea, all the world – for which Faustus hath lost both
> Germany and the world, yea heaven itself, heaven the
> seat of God, the throne of the blessed, the kingdom
> of joy, and must remain in hell for ever. Hell, ah
> hell for ever! Sweet friends, what shall become of
> Faustus, being in hell for ever? (Sc. xix.45–51)

Even in his very last scene Faustus is reminded that he still has an 'amiable soul' which can be saved if he will 'call for mercy and avoid despair.'

> I see an angel hovers o'er thy head,
> And with a vial full of precious grace
> Offers to pour the same into thy soul. (Sc. xviii.60–63)

But Faustus is never able to overcome his hopelessness: 'I do repent and yet I do despair.' His feelings are the result of his inadequate faith. His despair is a consequence of his doubt that God can or will find him worthy of forgiveness. And this, in turn, is a direct consequence of his perverse pride in his extreme behavior as an overreacher. To doubt that he can be saved is to doubt that grace is freely given. And to doubt that grace is freely given, to lack faith, makes Faustus's repentance worthless. Though one drop of precious grace would save him, he will be denied that drop: 'See, see where Christ's blood streams in the firmament!/ One drop would save my soul, half a drop! Ah, my Christ!'

---

[20] *Institutes*, I. xiv. 18; Sinfield, p. 118.

The deity depicted in *Doctor Faustus* is neither so generous nor so merciful that He will save the despairing scholar. Little if any of the New Testament's compassion, charity, and forgiveness seem exercised here. Faustus, the overreacher, finds not signs of love and welcome but rather gestures of rejection and condemnation: 'And see where God/ Stretches out his arms and bends his ireful brows.' In fact, this deity seems to be still another absolute and unyielding power, like Tamburlaine when his tents are colored black. This sense of the Christian God seen as severe and legalistic, aloof and unresponsive, may reflect something of the religious controversy we considered earlier. Perhaps the God of Protestantism – Faustus was, after all, educated at Wittenberg, a city closely identified with Luther – might well seem remote and forbidding. In contrast to Catholicism, Protestantism provides none of the comfort or reassurance of auricular confession and priestly absolution. In addition, a suppliant could no longer appeal to the panoply of saints for special assistance nor ask the Mother of God to intercede on one's behalf. The Protestant worshipper addresses God directly, a God who, according to Luther, demands absolute faith alone and who, according to the Calvinist doctrine of the Elect, has predestined from birth those who will be saved and those who will not. Faustus describes a God who judges him with 'heavy wrath,' like the Scythian shepherd with the Virgins of Damascus.

But, in fact, the play does not seem to support any specific religion. The assurances of the Good Angel and the Old Man are surely genuine and suggest that the hero is not absolutely predestined to die a reprobate. Furthermore, the suspense and excitement aroused by the drama are due to our hope that he might well accept these offers and save himself. This overreacher can always release his grasp and settle for the lot common to all humanity. The poetry, too, heightens our awareness of the powerful feelings that lie behind the words: 'Rend not my heart for naming of my Christ!/ Yet will I call on him. O spare me, Lucifer!' 'My God, my God, look not so fierce on me!' The play can only succeed on the stage when the audience is convinced of the real possibility that Faustus may deny his thirst to exceed the mortal, reform, repent, and believe.

Marlowe further complicates the characterization of the overreacher by showing Faustus as an individual of extraordinary promise whose abilities, so far above those of the common man, are ultimately worthless, for he accomplishes nothing. Striving to be more than a man, he ends ironically desiring to be less:

> This soul should fly from me and I be changed
> Unto some brutish beast. All beasts are happy.
> For, when they die
> Their souls are soon dissolved in elements,
> But mine must live still to be plagued in hell.   (Sc. xix.175–179)

The overreacher who has lived only for his own satisfaction, who could acknowledge nothing beyond his own ego, has spent his time 'in pleasure and in dalliance.' We learn that self-indulgence is a debilitating practice, as we watch the steady degeneration of Faustus. In the course of the action the scenes of low comedy are not kept separate from the Faustus story but gradually become an integral part of it as Faustus himself becomes one of the clowns and practical jokers. Surely our sense of the tragic in *Doctor Faustus* results, in part, from our sense of loss and waste.

We experience this sense of loss and waste because the man who had the capacity to achieve so much has achieved nothing. The delights of this life have proved ultimately transient, destructive, and illusory, like the demonic spirit in the guise of Helen who assures the ultimate damnation of Faustus. At the end, Faustus has risked all for what he finally realizes is frivolous. But when he turns away from the pleasure and dalliance of the temporal world as valueless pastimes, he finds that the rewards of the spiritual world can be secured only by what seems to him to be absolute subservience, a demeaning abasement of the self to a tyrannical and vengeful deity. In short, it seems that the individual can achieve nothing worthwhile on his own, and his salvation in the next world requires a total denial of the self. The tragedy, then, is not simply that as in *Tamburlaine* man must die, but that man cannot live or expect in the afterlife anything that will allow him dignity and self-esteem.

Marlowe's overreachers are doomed to lives of frustration. They can never satisfy the ambition that drives them or resolve their discontent with the human condition. Ironically, they seek a glory that forever escapes them. They are, appropriately, fit subjects for tragedy. But man's frustrations, his inability to accommodate means and ends, need not always be regarded as tragic. After all, that one cannot cut one's garment to fit one's cloth reveals an inadequacy potentially as laughable as it is serious. These differences in point of view can be accounted for in part by an individual playwright's personal temperament and in part by the society for which he wrote. For example, that Marlowe and Jonson saw human nature by radically different lights and that some twenty years separated *Tamburlaine* and *Doctor Faustus* from *The Alchemist* are facts that help explain the world of difference between them. As Edward Partridge has observed:

> Even as Marlowe dramatized the glamour, the aspirations, and some of the dangers of the Elizabethan Age, so Jonson dramatized the aftermath of the aspirations that were never realized and the glamour that could never be more than ideal. He saw the obscene and ludicrous underside of the great heroes of the past. ... The vast world of Tamburlaine or Faustus was narrowed down to a London house during the plague or to Smithfield during the Fair.[21]

Unlike Marlowe, Jonson intended his plays in part as moral correctives for his audience. In the prologues to *Volpone*, *Epicoene*, and *The Alchemist* he

---

[21] *The Broken Compass, A Study in the Major Comedies of Ben Jonson*, p. 236.

claims that art should 'mix profit with ... pleasure,' and give 'wholesome remedies' and 'fair correctives' to the ills of society 'by writing ... things, like truth, well feigned.' And so Jonson's characters are not fashioned according to Pico's conception of mankind, idealized and heroic, nor are they tragic in their defeat. Rather, they are rogues and fools, the butt of satiric laughter. Although some have appetites nearly as gigantesque as those of Tamburlaine and Faustus, most are hungry not because of a taste for glory but because of greed.

In *The Alchemist*, we are shown that insatiable greed is the most common failing of humanity, emblematic of man's fallen state; it is found in everyone. By presenting a series of portraits demonstrating how avarice affects the behavior of all mankind, Jonson establishes its prevalence and paints a background for his later picture of the overreacher. First, we meet those lesser specimens whose greed is all too human in scale. Dapper seems a modest lawyer's clerk, 'the sole hope of his old grandmother,' who begins by seeking 'A rifling fly' to play 'at horses, and winne cups.' But tantalized by the hope of gain, he soon professes to require 'a great familiar ... for all games,' and will not be content until he is blest as the nephew to the Queen of Fairy so that he can 'win up all the money i' the town.' He is eventually found starved and nearly asphyxiated in a privy, stripped of all valuables – even the gold half-crown, a token from his former love – and left with only a worthless charm – a 'leaden heart' he has worn ever since his love forsook him. Another specimen of petty humanity with outsized aspirations is Abel Drugger, the young tobacconist who 'would be glad to thrive.' He starts by requesting business advice and ends by expecting to marry a rich widow. He, too, is bilked and disappointed.

But these examples of human weakness, which are easily multiplied, are too typical of mankind, too commonplace to serve as examples of the overreacher. For such a figure, larger-than-life size dimensions are required, and these are supplied by the portrait of Sir Epicure Mammon. This knight is endowed with all the qualities found in the Marlovian overreacher. Mammon, indeed, possesses the energy and exuberance, the boundless taste for life we have found in Tamburlaine and Faustus. Desiring Herculean stamina, he demonstrates a colossal egotism and an arrogant self-confidence that recall both the Scythian shepherd and the wonder-working doctor.[22]

Sir Epicure Mammon will, so he claims, lead the way like Tamburlaine into the 'Nove orbe,' the new world. This new world is a golden one, for gold is to Mammon what power is to Tamburlaine or knowledge to Faustus. Once possessed of the alchemist's stone, Mammon will turn all of

---

[22] 'Mammon is a Faustus of the senses, captivated by the dreams of exploring the utmost possibilities of recondite and exquisite sensation, as Faustus by the dream of boundless knowledge and power. The sordid Mephistophiles of the laboratory never fulfills his bond, but Mammon has already taken possession of his kingdom, and feasts full at the orgies his imagination provides.' C. H. Herford and Percy Simpson, *Ben Jonson*, Vol. II, p. 105.

life into a golden experience. For example, preparing to woo Dol Common, who is disguised as a mad noblewoman, Sir Epicure promises himself to

> talk to her all in gold;
> Rain her as many showers as Jove did drops
> Unto his Danaë; show the god a miser
> Compared with Mammon. What! the stone will do't.
> She shall feel gold, taste gold, sleep gold;
> Nay, we will concumbere gold. (IV.i.25–30)

Like Faustus's curiosity, the range of Mammon's concerns is vast, of epic dimensions. If he acquired the stone, he would rid the world of sickness and disease, making healthy the ill and restoring youth and potency to the elderly. His friends would thrive and the country would profit by his building new colleges, schools, hospitals, 'now and then, a church,' and by his even providing the marriage dowries for young virgins. Just as Faustus had planned to 'wall all Germany with brass/ And make swift Rhine circle fair Wittenberg,' so Mammon had expected to reconstruct London with

> a ditch about it
> Of silver; should have run with cream from Hogsden;
> That every Sunday in Moorfields the younkers
> And tits and tom-boys should have fed on, gratis. (V.v.77–80)

When the jig is up, when Lovewit has returned to claim possession of the goods in his house, when Subtle and Dol Common have fled over the back garden wall and Face has reverted to his role as Jeremy, the butler, then Sir Epicure takes some refuge behind his pretense to high moral intention:

> Lovewit: What a great loss in hope have you sustained!
> Mammon: Not I; the commonwealth has. (V.v.75–76)

Yet Mammon was never truly motivated by these proposals for the public benefit. In fact, when not fully possessed by imagination, he was aware that no commonwealth would accept him as a citizen. Dol Common wisely points out that no prince could permit a private individual to control the country's economy by making gold: 'O, but beware, sir! you may come to end/ The remnant of your days in a loath'd prison.' In response, Mammon proposes that they will take refuge in some free state, a Switzerland or Venice. But his haven sounds less like any real republic than a return to an age of gold – in which that metal is actually present, not simply a metaphor:

> We'll therefore go with all, my girl, and live
> In a free state, where we will eat our mullets
> Soused in high-country wines, sup pheasants' eggs,
> And have our cockles boiled in silver shells,
> Our shrimps to swim again, as when they lived,
> In a rare butter made of dolphins' milk,

> Whose cream does look like opals; and with these
> Delicate meats set ourselves high for pleasure.   (IV.i.155–162)

Indeed, Sir Epicure's civic-mindedness was always an illusion, for he would pervert all of society to serve his own pleasure, transforming fathers and mothers into bawds, husbands into cuckolds, clergymen into sycophants, politicians into puppets, men-about-town into eunuchs to 'fan me with ten ostrich tails/ Apiece, made in a plume to gather wind.' Even when he proposes to help others, he does so only to gratify his own lusts or ego:

> This is the day, wherein to all my friends,
> I will pronounce the happy word, 'Be Rich.'
> This day you shall be spectatissimi.   (II.i.6–8)

All his powers would be turned to his private use, and, typical of the overreacher's egotism, all would reflect the image of himself he wishes to see. In fact, although the inexhaustible drive found in Tamburlaine and Faustus exists in Mammon, the knight's particular interests are not gratified by power or knowledge but rather by physical passion: to 'enjoy a perpetuity/ Of life and lust.'

> I do mean
> To have a list of wives and concubines
> Equal with Solomon, who had the stone
> Alike with me; and I will make me a back
> With the elixir, that shall be as stout
> As Hercules', to encounter fifty a night.   (II.ii.34–39)

Everywhere he seeks his own image infinitely reflected, delighting in endless, rare, and exquisite sensual pleasures:

> I will have my beds blown up, not stuffed:
> Down is too hard. And then mine oval room
> Filled with such pictures as Tiberius took
> From Elephantis, and dull Aretine
> But coldly imitated. Then, my glasses
> Cut in more subtle angles, to disperse
> And multiply the figures as I walk
> Naked between my succubae. My mists
> I'll have of perfume, vapored 'bout the room,
> To loose our selves in; and my baths like pits
> To fall into; from whence we will come forth
> And roll us dry in gossamer and roses.   (II.ii.41–52)

Mammon is the overreacher as voluptuary. His flaw is recognized by his dupers, whose great art is to let each of their clients act out and pay for his own fantasy. While attempting to seduce Dol Common, Sir Epicure is revealed for what his name suggests. His pose as an altruistic dreamer is shown to be a pretense. Since the stone can be held only by one pure in spirit, Subtle and Face claim the knight has lost all, and Mammon acknowledges his own failing in a rare moment of near-tragic recognition:

'O, my voluptuous mind! I am justly punished ... By mine own base affections.'

Like all overreachers, Sir Epicure is destroyed by his own compulsion. He possesses greatness of appetite without the greatness of soul that should attend it. Mammon knows nothing of the 'magnanimity' that Tamburlaine praises or Perkins decries. Rather than follow Pico's injunction to 'pant after the highest and ... toil with all our strength to obtain it,' rather than imitate Faustus who would 'tire thy brains to get a deity,' Mammon pants in ecstasy after physical pleasures. In fact, the extraordinary efforts he intends to make to achieve exotic delights in sex and food are nearly the only subject-matter of his conversation. Idealism and altruism are not a part of his nature. Given absolute freedom to become what he will, Jonsonian man in general will be dominated by narrow self-interest: he is a fallen creature. But although man may be fallen, the universe is not. As Gabriele Bernhard Jackson points out:

> There are certain actions the universe itself will not permit: 'No lye ever growes old.' The universe is truthful. Further, 'no ill can happen to a good man. Contraries are not mixed.' The universe is just; the universe is consistent. Nature, the administrator on earth of this divine impulse toward truth, directs earthly affairs in such a way that nothing determined by her presents an appearance that does not correspond to its reality; furthermore, she brings to light any attempted deceit.[23]

Sir Epicure leaves the stage defeated, claiming that he will 'mount a turnip-cart and preach/ The end o'th world, within these two months.' But in his bitter disappointment, he shows no trace of understanding that his greed has been the cause of his downfall. Mammon, the overreacher, holds himself in such high esteem that he cannot accept his own responsibility for his victimization. His extreme pessimism is only the obverse of the extreme optimism he voiced earlier. He has learned nothing; and, no doubt, soon prompted by self-interest, he will once again be ripe for the cony-catchers of the age.

The overreacher by his very nature is doomed to frustration; his aspirations will always exceed his ability. He is incapable of understanding that happiness can come from acknowledging the weaknesses of humankind, accepting human limitations, and exercising moderation and restraint. Heeding the kind of exhortation for self-fulfillment found in Pico very often leaves the overreacher friendless, alone, and dissatisfied. The Neoplatonist argued that mankind is capable of becoming demi-gods – emulating the angels in dignity and glory. But in Renaissance drama, those who attempt this, end as tragic heroes or satiric butts. Although the effort to achieve angelic dignity and glory may be thrilling in its demonstration of the power of man's will, the results for Marlowe's and Jonson's heroes are ultimately disappointing.

---

[23] Gabriele Bernhard Jackson, *Vision and Judgment in Ben Jonson's Drama*, p. 55. Jonson's sentences are quoted from his *Discoveries*, p. 542, and pp. 9–10 of the Herford and Simpson edition.

In *The Tempest*, Shakespeare presents a rather different view of the over-reacher, for his hero has come to understand that happiness is best attained not by exceeding the human but by embodying it fully. By dedicating himself to the acquisition of superhuman power, Prospero has lost his position and his country. Although Duke of Milan, he preferred to remain in his library, withdrawing from his proper responsibility: 'to my state grew stranger, being transported/ And rapt in secret studies.' He became, in fact a *roi fainéant*, a monarch who ruled largely in name, preferring to leave the business of government to his deputy.[24] So Prospero's brother, Antonio, was chosen to run affairs of state that were properly Prospero's own concern. In this way, the rightful Duke of Milan, 'thus neglecting worldly ends, all dedicated/ To closeness and the bettering of my mind/ With that which .../ O'er priz'd all popular rate,' lost the dukedom to his usurping surrogate. Of course, Prospero was wrong to turn over to another the duties that were his alone, though Antonio was even more wrong to seize power in his own name and endanger the lives of Prospero and Miranda.

Although Prospero's studies have resulted in the loss of his dukedom, they have given him remarkable power. He himself can order those spirits by whose aid the sun, the sea, the thunder and lightning obey his words:

> I have bedimm'd
> The noontide sun, call'd forth the mutinous winds,
> And 'twixt the green sea and the azur'd vault
> Set roaring war: to the dread rattling thunder
> Have I given fire, and rifted Jove's stout oak
> With his own bolt　　　　　　　　　　　　　(V.i.41–46)

He has even achieved what Faustus considers the ultimate goal of medicine, to give life to the dead: 'graves at my command/ Have wak'd their sleepers, op'd, and let 'em forth.' He has freed Ariel from the torments inflicted through the black magic of Sycorax, the witch, and he has controlled her son, Caliban, who acts on only the most savage instincts until his last speech in the play promises something of a reformation. Both Ariel, the spirit of fire and air, and the reptilian, fishy-smelling Caliban, a creature of earth and water, must do as Prospero commands. Finally. with his 'so potent Art,' he can force his enemies to acknowledge his superior abilities, return his dukedom – and even bring some of them to ask forgiveness. With all these powers, Prospero can perhaps be regarded as the best dramatic embodiment of Pico's ideals – an overreacher for the noblest causes.

But to gain these extraordinary abilities, he has paid a high price, for he and his daughter have been cut off from mankind, enisled in the company

---

[24] For a discussion of the concept of the *roi fainéant* see Roger Lockyer, *Buckingham, The Life and Political Career of George Villiers.*

of what is below the human (Caliban) or above it (Ariel). The ambition that drove Prospero to spend years of study in his cell acquiring super-human ability through magic did not reward him with happiness. At the first opportunity he readily exchanges power as a magician for political power; he chooses to resume his rightful place in the world of men. To return to society, to resume his place, Prospero must not only defeat his enemies but also cast aside his magic, burying his staff and drowning his book. These acts, demonstrating his rejection of his powers as an over-reacher, paradoxically prove that Prospero has now acquired still another kind of knowledge, the wisdom and understanding that enables him to exercise his 'nobler reason' and to grant forgiveness:

> Though with their high wrongs I am struck to th'quick,
> Yet with my nobler reason, 'gainst my fury
> Do I take part: the rarer action is
> In virtue than in vengeance: they being penitent,
> The sole drift of my purpose doth extend
> Not a frown further. (V.i.25–30)

This exercise of 'nobler reason,' of 'virtue' rather than revenge is further evidence that Prospero has recovered from the self-indulgence that allowed him to devote himself totally to his studies. After a dozen years on the island, he now abjures· magic forever and demonstrates the self-discipline and self-control that will enable him to sail to Italy as ruler of Milan:

> For you, most wicked sir, whom to call brother
> Would even infect my mouth, I do forgive
> Thy rankest fault, – all of them; and require
> My dukedom of thee, which perforce, I know
> Thou must restore. (V.i.129–134)

His decision must reflect what he has come to understand after his years in exile. Like all overreachers, Prospero was clearly not contented. But Pros-pero's discontentment was not the result of frustrated aspirations, that goad for all other overreachers. Instead, his unhappiness was the result of his own failure to be human. Prospero discovers that man's happiness must come not from his denial but rather from his acceptance of human limitations, from his holding values and fulfilling responsibilities that alone can make man's estate rewarding. Actually, this is a view of man closer to Hooker's position than Pico's or Calvin's. In The Tempest, Prospero tells his listeners what those values are for him. First among these is sympathetic understanding, a compassion that enables him to respond to human feeling. Ariel, a pure spirit of air, is so moved by the sorrow of those punished that he encourages Prospero to sympathize:

> Ariel: The king,
>   His brother, and yours, abide all three distracted,
>   And the remainder mourning over them,
>   Brimful of sorrow and dismay; but chiefly

Him you term'd, sir, 'The good old lord, Gonzalo';
His tears runs down his beard, like winter's drops
From eaves of reeds. Your charm so strongly works 'em,
That if you now beheld them, your affections
Would become tender.
Prosp: Dost thou think so, spirit?
Ariel: Mine would, sir, were I human.
Prosp: And mine shall.
Hast thou, which art but air, a touch, a feeling
Of their afflictions, and shall not myself,
One of their kind, that relish all as sharply
Passion as they, be kindlier mov'd than thou art?

(V.i.11–24)

In addition to exercising the 'rarer action' of forgiveness, Prospero knows as well the 'soft grace' that comes with patience, stoic resignation, and acceptance. With her 'sovereign aid,' Prospero can 'rest myself content' – experiencing a comfort unavailable to the overreacher. Prospero further acknowledges that he lives not for his own self-indulgence, not for the gratification of his own ego, but rather finds happiness in the happiness of his child. He tells her fiancé:

If I have too austerely punish'd you,
Your compensation makes amends; for I
Have given you here a third of mine own life,
Or that for which I live.   (IV.i.1–4)

Finally, by resuming his proper role in society, by governing as 'Absolute Milan,' Prospero will give definition and usefulness to his existence. He will follow Hooker's advice to hold to the due ordering of things. Unlike Tamburlaine, Prospero can prepare himself for the inevitable: in Milan, 'Every third thought shall be my grave.' Prospero knows the importance of both the active and the contemplative life: how one lives it and how one prepares for leaving it are equally important.

To sum up: cultivating empathy, forgiveness, and patience as well as accepting the weaknesses of humanity are the ways one lives happily in society. Practicing self-discipline, fulfilling a responsible position, giving loving attention to the future of one's children, and preparing for the life to come are how one lives happily as an individual. Rejecting Pico's fable that man is capable of attaining any height, even a successful overreacher, a wonder-working mage, cannot be content to leave behind his own humanity and the society of his fellows. Tamburlaine, Faustus, and Sir Epicure demonstrate that man is incapable of attaining the overreacher's dream of glory; Prospero teaches us that man is incapable of enjoying that dream even if he could attain it.

In contrast to these earlier overreachers, the aspirations of those in the later Jacobean theater are considerably diminished. Mankind is not pre-

sented by the dramatists of this period as a being capable of pursuing
far-ranging goals. Perhaps the growing influence of the Puritans convinced
writers that humanity was not only fallen and corrupt but also weak and
damned. Boundless freedom of action seems unimaginable.

Perhaps, too, the numerous and rapid shifts in the social status of individuals and families commonplace at this time, a consequence of the
practices of James's rule and of the general economic conditions of the
period, left dramatists feeling that extraordinary strength of character was
not necessary to rise to positions of power in society. Since numerous
examples of those who suddenly acquired high titles or vast wealth were
well known, what might once have seemed a phenomenon was now only
a customary occurrence, and such occurrences do not require overreachers to enact them.

As a consequence of the looser economic and social fabric and of the
increasing dominance of the Puritans with their darker and narrower view
of man's possibilities, a dramatist writing for the public theaters in the first
quarter of the seventeenth century could present a more realistic portrait
of the overreacher, one who resembled his precursors in a single characteristic only: his intensity, the fervor with which he pursues his greatly
reduced aims. The mythic, larger-than-life dimensions of the earlier overreacher have shrunk to the all-too-human. Only his perseverance and his
unflagging energy and determination remain. Indeed, the most impressive overreacher in the drama of the late Jacobean period is loosely based
on an historical figure: Sir Giles Mompesson, the ruthless financier
and scoundrel who becomes Massinger's Sir Giles Overreach.[25] This
thoroughgoing villain in *A New Way To Pay Old Debts* is presented as a heart-
less but industrious social climber, one who wants to make his only child
a great lady. He does not aspire to conquer any worlds or scale any
heavens; he has no desire to work wonders. He does not even care greatly
for high social position for himself! He is identifiable as an overreacher not
by the greatness of his ambition, but by his name and by the intense
compulsion that drives him ultimately to terrifying madness.

As we have seen, earlier embodiments of the overreacher were presented either in Tamburlaine-like fashion as a man above the law, or as
such men as Faustus, Sir Epicure Mammon, or Prospero who were more
harmful to themselves than to others. But Massinger's version of this
character type is intentionally villainous in the pursuit of his goal. Evil and
powerful, Sir Giles combines 'a spirit to dare and power to do.' He will
force those who will not sell their property to such legal expenses that

---

[25] For the stage history of this character see Robert Hamilton Ball, *The Amazing Career of Sir Giles
Overreach*. I have used the edition of the play prepared by Philip Edwards and Colin Gibson in
The Plays and Poems of Philip Massinger, Vol. II. This most recent publication of Massinger's
complete works favors a later date for this play than that proposed by the Harbage-
Schoenbaum *Annals*, and these editors argue that Sir Giles is not a 'specific caricature' of
Mompesson. See especially pp. 273–278.

they will be broken by court costs and so part with their land for half the value. Rather than help friends and relatives who are down on their fortunes, he would set his 'feet/ Upon their heads to press 'em to the bottom.' His reputation is a matter of complete indifference to him:

> when my ears are pierced with widows' cries,
> And undone orphans wash with tears my threshold,
> I only think what 'tis to have my daughter
> Right honorable; and 'tis a powerful charm
> Makes me insensible of remorse or pity
> Or the least sting of conscience.   (IV.i.126–131)

Sir Giles is interested neither in the power that money brings nor in the glory of wealth and riches but in the social status of his only child: 'All my ambition is to have my daughter/ Right honorable.'

> Why, foolish girl, was't not to make thee great
> That I have ran, and still pursue, those ways
> That hale down curses on me, which I mind not?
> Part with these humble thoughts, and apt thyself
> To the noble state I labor to advance thee,
> Or by my hopes to see thee honorable,
> I will adopt a stranger to my heir,
> And throw thee from my care.   (III.ii.54–61)

His warning recalls the phrasing of Lear's rejection of Cordelia, 'new-adopted to our hate'; 'as a stranger to my heart and me/ Hold thee from this for ever.' And perhaps the madness that ultimately overtakes Sir Giles is somewhat inspired by this famous example of a father who felt betrayed by his daughter and who suffers the loss of his sanity. Yet, Sir Giles's blank verse has none of the ferocity of Lear's poetry, even if something of the old king's words echoed in the back of Massinger's mind as he wrote. Indeed, nowhere is his language as rich in metaphor or as ripe in comparisons and allusions as that of the earlier overreachers we considered.

Nevertheless earlier versions of the overreacher may also have influenced Massinger in the concluding scene of his play. When Sir Giles with drawn sword attempts to kill his child, he imitates Tamburlaine who actually slays Calyphas, the son who failed him. And in his last words, Sir Giles recalls the hysteria, madness, and terror of Doctor Faustus:

> Ha! What are these? Sure, hangmen
> That come to bind my hands, and then to drag me
> Before the judgment seat. Now they are new shapes,
> And do appear like Furies, with steel whips
> To scourge my ulcerous soul. Shall I then fall
> Ingloriously, and yield? No; spite of fate,
> I will be forced to hell like to myself.
> Though you were legions of accursed spirits,
> Thus would I fly among you.   (V.i.365–373)

Massinger concludes his drama with a moral injunction that is both banal and shallow:

Here is a precedent to teach wicked men
That when they leave religion and turn atheists,
Their own abilities leave 'em.   (V.i.379–381)

This 'precedent' is also somewhat surprising, for the play has taught no
such lesson. In fact, the work never mentions the importance of religion
of any kind or sect, nor has it discussed the dangers of atheism. The play
does not really raise profound questions about how life should be lived or
propose a view of human nature based on a philosophical or spiritual
conception of man. Diminished in his spiritual capacity, the overreacher
lacks the will to aspire to more than human greatness or the imagination
to dream of superhuman achievements.

These faint echoes of earlier stage figures – betrayed, crazed, murderous, and damned – who all seem to contribute to the portrait of Sir Giles,
suggest that this overreacher lacks not only the boundless aspiration and
thrilling language but also the individuality and stature of his predecessors. We are left to ask what becomes of such a diminished being.
Actually, this new, lesser breed is of hardy stock. As Marlowe's overreachers set the pattern for the idealized fighters, the Almanzors and
Aureng-Zebes, of late seventeenth century heroic tragedies, so Massinger's Sir Giles ultimately became the prototype for the two-dimensional
villains of nineteenth century melodrama, deaf to widows' cries and unmoved by orphans' tears, driven only by a desire for mercenary reward or
social standing.

V

The Machiavel and
The Tool Villain

The tool villain, the simple henchman who carries out the orders of his employer, begins his dramatic career as a supporting player, a rather insignificant stock figure hired and eventually discarded by the Machiavel he serves. Indeed, Machiavels, disciples of Machiavelli, clever, ruthless, and powerful manipulators of men and society, can even be recognized by their use of such an assistant. As the Machiavel became a frequent leading character in the drama at the turn of the century, the tool villain appeared at his side ready to do his bidding for gold, promotion, or at least the promise of such rewards.[1] But this agent for evil does not remain long without a personality of his own. The stages in the development of the tool villain as a distinctive character in English Renaissance drama can be appreciated first by examining what may be the two earliest representatives in the Elizabethan theater, those found in Kyd's The Spanish Tragedy (1587) and in Marlowe's The Jew of Malta (1589). We shall then consider two who appear in Shakespeare's plays; more coherently created versions of the type, one is from a relatively early work, Richard III (1593), and the other from a late romance, The Winter's Tale (1610). And, finally, we shall look at two later Jacobean examples, from Webster's The Duchess of Malfi (1614) and from Middleton and Rowley's The Changeling (1622). By studying these plays we shall be able to trace the evolution of the tool villain from a rather colorless minor player, one whose chief characteristic is that he has no conscience, into a major character who reveals considerable depth and complexity.

Since the Machiavel calls him into being, the tool villain's origins can be found by analyzing the practices of those whose machinations make use of him. Such men, devious and fearless, were believed to be pupils of Niccolò Machiavelli, the Florentine historian and political theoretician. Knowledge of Machiavelli's writings, including The Prince and the Discourses,

---

[1] According to Wyndham Lewis in The Lion and the Fox, p. 65, Mr Edward Meyer 'has catalogued three hundred and ninety-five references to Machiavelli in elizabethan literature.'

reached some Elizabethans in the sixteenth century even though the publication of these books, which were considered shocking and controversial, was banned in England.[2] Copies in the original Italian as well as in French and Latin translations crossed the Channel and were read avidly, arousing admiration in some and horror in others.[3] But the general public's notion of Machiavelli came from the Frenchman, Innocent Gentillet, author of the Contra-Machiavel (1576), a widely circulated book so exaggerating Machiavelli's ideas that his reputation as an atheistic and totally immoral writer became permanently set in the minds of those who had never read him.[4] The result was that the Gentillet version of Machiavelli's politician was assimilated into English drama as a kind of Senecan criminal-hero who, for good measure, also incorporated into his nature some of the character traits of the Vice of the Morality plays. As a consequence, the Machiavel was a formidable combination of evils. Bernard Spivack sums up the effect of Machiavelli and his interpreters on the theater:

> By propounding the technique of worldly success without regards to any higher allegiance, Machiavelli elevated the most serious defect of human nature, from a Christian viewpoint, into a positive achievement. By defining power as the prize available to certain natural qualities he dissolved its divine auspices. By creating political science he abolished the religious principle in human society. The Elizabethans really understood him well enough, and indeed their traditional values within their transitional age taught them to apprehend the evil before they were actually aware of the man who later lent it his name. On their stage the Machiavellian villain, through his egotism, his ruthless energy unhampered by pious restraints, his deliberate disavowal of any law higher than his own appetite, his penetrating and cynical awareness of the animal impulses composing man's lower nature, enacts the thrust of the new realism against the traditional Christian sanctities applicable to the life of this world. Legitimacy, order, honor, love, and the stable community of human creatures under God are the easy obstacles his purposes surmount because the pieties and simplicities of honest men render them defenceless against his policy. It is a rare villain in the drama of that time who is not in some degree a Machiavel. ... The age was aware of Machiavellianism before it was aware of Machiavelli.[5]

Although Machiavelli's actual influence may be sometimes hard to detect in the stage character of the Machiavel, the theoretical principles set forth in The Prince clearly define how the villain is treated in the drama. In Chapter 19, which discusses how a ruler may avoid being hated by his

---

[2] See F. Raab, The English Face of Machiavelli; Mario Praz, 'Machiavelli and the Elizabethans,' Proceedings of the British Academy XIII (1928); Hardin Craig, The Enchanted Glass.

[3] See J. W. Allen, Political Thought in the 16th Century, p. 440, ft. 3. The Prince was first published in Italian in 1532, in French in 1551, and in Latin in 1560.

[4] Gentillet was first translated into English and published by Simon Patericke: A Discourse Upon the Wel Governing and Maintaining in Good Peace, a Kingdome, or other principalitie. Against Nicholas Machiavel the Florentine (London, 1602).

[5] Shakespeare and the Allegory of Evil, pp. 375–376.

subjects, Machiavelli proposes that a prince 'delegate to others those measures which entail blame, to himself those which cause pleasure.'[6] This advice concerning the usefulness of a tool villain is illustrated with a specific example in Chapter 7. There the author relates with approval how Caesare Borgia appointed the Spanish captain, Don Ramiro de Lorqua, as the governor of the Romagna with absolute authority to accomplish its unification and pacification. Those aims achieved, Caesare dissociated himself from the harshness of Ramiro's administration: 'so once he got the opportunity, he had Ramiro's body laid out one morning in two pieces in the public square at Cesna with a block of wood and a bloody sword beside it. The brutalty of this spectacle left those people simultaneously gratified and terrified.'[7] Ultimately, as this example proves, the tool villain seldom receives the reward he expects, and Ramiro's fate establishes the pattern for this figure's treatment.

Gentillet, too, related this incident, but as an instance of the immorality of Machiavelli's ruler:

> A Prince which will exercise some cruell and rigorous act (Saith M. Nicholas) hee ought to give the commission thereof unto some other, to the end, he may not acquire evill will and enmitie by it. And yet if he feare that such a delegation cannot be wholly exempted from blame (to have consented to the execution which was made by his Commissarie) he may cause the Commissarie to bee slaine, to shewe that he consented not to his crueltie, as did *Caesar Borgia*, and *Messire Remiro Dorco*.[8]

Like Machiavelli, Gentillet presents this example both as typical behavior for a successful ruler who is a disciple of the Florentine and as the usual fate of the tool villain whose life ends once he is no longer useful to the prince he serves.[9]

The principle of using a subordinate who can later be blamed to accomplish necessary but unpopular actions was well understood by the Elizabethans. Heeding Machiavelli's advice, Sir Walter Raleigh adopts the principle in his *Maxims of State* that to retain popularity with his subjects, a ruler should 'commit the handling of such things as procure envy, or seem grevious to his ministers, but reserve those things which are gratefull and well pleasing to himself.'[10] And in dealing with other countries, a ruler should follow Raleigh's precept: he should hold blameworthy the agent commissioned with accomplishing what is desired by the prince but threatening to others:

---

[6] *The Prince*, translated and edited by James B. Atkinson, p. 295.

[7] P. 167.

[8] III.*34. Quoted by Fredson Bowers in 'Kyd's Pedringano: Sources and Parallels,' *Harvard Studies and Notes in Philology and Literature* (1931), 13:241–249.

[9] In II*33 Gentillet describes how the Machiavellian prince will 'put those to death who helped him to the crown.'

[10] *The Complete Works*, edited by Oldys and Birch, Vol. VIII, p. 15.

If any thing [is] to be done not justifiable, or unfit to be allowed, as oftentimes it happeneth, there to lay the blame upon the minister; which must be performed with so great show of revenge and dissimulation, by reproving and punishing the minister, as the [foreign] prince offended may be satisfied, and believe that the cause of unkindness proceeded from thence.[11]

Accordingly, Raleigh endorses the tool villain as a sound means for a ruler to shield his own reputation and still achieve what he wishes in matters involving both national and international affairs. Not to be left far behind, Bacon discusses some of the advantages of this strategy in his essay 'Of Simulation and Dissimulation.'

In English Renaissance drama, Lorenzo, in Thomas Kyd's *The Spanish Tragedy*, is surely among the earliest of Machiavellian villains. Nephew to the King of Spain, Lorenzo intends to accomplish his own advancement by marrying his sister, Bel-imperia, to Balthazar, the Prince of Portugal. With Balthazar's help Lorenzo organizes the murder of Horatio, her current suitor. In this action Lorenzo imitates Machiavelli's two favorite animals, the lion and the fox, using equal measures of force and guile: '*tam armis quam ingenio*: Where words prevail not, violence prevails,' he exclaims. His plans for self-advancement, ruthlessly carried out, are based on Machiavellian tactics and expressed in Machiavellian jargon, for he talks of 'policy,' 'complots,' and 'practices,' terms especially associated with Florentine politics. Bel-imperia's happiness and Horatio's life are subjects unworthy of consideration.

As the complete Machiavel, Lorenzo naturally uses a tool villain. By flattery and bribery – 'store of gold coin,/ And lands and living join'd with dignities' – he makes an agent of Pedringano, Bel-imperia's servant. From him, Lorenzo and Balthazar learn whom Bel-imperia favors and where the lovers meet. With Pedringano and Serberine, a servant of Balthazar's, the four men interrupt the lovers' tryst, forcibly carry off Bel-imperia, and kill Horatio. Now Lorenzo has only to persuade his sister of the good sense in returning Balthazar's love for her. In the meantime, however, Lorenzo orders Pedringano to shoot Serberine, whom Lorenzo accuses of being untrustworthy. Lorenzo sets up the assassination in such a way that the watch is conveniently on hand to arrest Pedringano. And so by his stratagem, Lorenzo removes both his accomplices: 'Thus must we practise to prevent mishap,/ And thus one ill another must expulse.'

The trick of using one 'ill' to eliminate another is a favorite operating principle of the Machiavel, and in this way the tool villain is often self-eliminating, for Lorenzo has no intention of helping the imprisoned Pedringano or of saving him from the rope. On the contrary, the tool villain's death will free Lorenzo entirely from the danger of blackmail or betrayal – or so he thinks.

---

[11] *The Cabinet-Council* in *Complete Works*, Vol. VIII, p. 51.

The hanging of Pedringano is managed by Kyd with a fine sense of dramatic irony and treated with sardonic humor – one might truly say 'gallows humor.' A young boy is sent to Pedringano to show him a box that according to Lorenzo contains a signed pardon and to encourage the condemned prisoner to 'be merry still.' As a test of his faith in Lorenzo, the tool villain is told he will be saved only at the very last moment. The messenger faithfully fulfills these orders, even though, once alone, he disobeys Lorenzo by secretly opening the box and discovering that it is empty:

> I must go to Pedringano, and tell him his pardon is in this box, nay, I would have sworn it, had I not seen the contrary. I cannot choose but smile to think how the villain will flout the gallows, scorn the audience, and descant on the hangman, and all presuming of his pardon from hence. Will't not be an odd jest, for me to stand and grace every jest he makes, pointing my finger at this box, as who would say, 'Mock on, here's thy warrant.' Is't not a scurvy jest, that a man should jest himself to death?　(III.v.8–17)

So Pedringano faces his judge with impudence and jokes with the executioner even as he is hanged. And all the while, of course, he keeps his eyes on and places his trust in 'yonder boy with the box in his hand.' He dies before he can publicly reveal Lorenzo's treachery and crimes. This incident is organized to demonstrate the inevitable self-deception of the tool villain. For Pedringano, as for most of the characters in this play, life is filled with dramatic irony: 'I know if need should be, my noble lord/ Will stand between me and ensuing harm' is a thought that Pedringano comes to realize is wrong only when it is too late. The macabre tone and the bitterness of the comedy, though striking, are appropriate for showing that honor is not to be found even among thieves – or, in this case, murderers. So Pedringano receives the reward of the tool villain, the reward that comes to anyone foolish enough to commit evil for the benefit of another. Still, he does not develop a distinctive personality. Rather, he remains the agent of the Machiavel, one who derives his identity from his function and not from his own nature.

Marlowe's Ithamore in *The Jew of Malta* is a tool villain considerably more developed. Unlike Pedringano, Ithamore has a personal history and independent emotional responses. And, also unlike Pedringano, this tool villain has obviously already found his way to villainy before he meets the Machiavel who employs him. Born in Thrace and reared in Arabia, Ithamore is sold as a slave by the Spaniards who have taken him prisoner. Once purchased by Barabas, the Machiavellian Jew of Malta, the tool villain quickly establishes his credentials by enumerating his crimes, which compare favorably with the activities of his master. Ithamore has spent his time 'In setting Christian villages on fire,/ Chaining of eunuchs, binding of gallye slaves,' murdering travelers, and crippling pilgrims. For his part, the Machiavel confesses that he has busied himself killing the sick, poisoning wells, baiting Christian thieves, practicing usury, and generally slaying 'friend and enemy with my strategems.' The two men are clearly well suited to each other.

As a tool villain, however, Ithamore serves the will of the Machiavel. He silences Abigail, Barabas's daughter, from telling one young man that she truly loves another, and he delivers challenges that lead these rivals to kill each other in a duel. He brings poisoned rice porridge that destroys an entire nunnery along with Abigail, who has joined the convent as a novice on the death of her sweetheart. Finally, Ithamore aids Barabas in the strangling of the Friar who has heard Abigail's deathbed confession. In some of this activity Ithamore even resembles Pedringano, for Kyd's tool villain also silences the heroine and carries her off to be confined, and he aids in the murder of Horatio, who is stabbed and hanged in a garden bower much as a Friar in Marlowe's play is hanged and strangled in the discovery space where he is found sleeping.[12]

One of Marlowe's most important contributions to the character type of the tool villain is that he gives this figure a personality of his own. In Marlowe's view, villainy knows no bounds, and Machiavels are neither exceptional nor rare. But as a tool villain, Ithamore is not simply a Machiavel's agent, for he has both a private past and a libidinous present. His attraction to the courtesan Bellamira turns him in Act IV into a money-hungry blackmailer of the Machiavel who owns him, and he repeatedly threatens Barabas with betrayal unless he furnishes larger and larger payments. Although Ithamore has neither the intelligence nor the cleverness to succeed in this endeavor, his independent action would have been unimaginable for Pedringano.

Marlowe even writes a parody of a love scene for the 'poor Turk of tenpence,' as Ithamore calls himself: 'That kiss again! She runs division of

---

[12] Actually, both plays are most alike in their tone, for they are dominated by a sardonic humour, grim, exaggerated, and sometimes even macabre. As we have seen, The Spanish Tragedy relies chiefly on dramatic irony for its effects; in this play words and deeds are in constant contradiction. For example, Bel-imperia praises the bower as an especially safe place for a lover's assignation, and Lorenzo congratulates himself that Pedringano's death will clear him of murder. The Jew of Malta, on the other hand, makes frequent use of the aside as a device to reveal the opposition between language and intention, words and meanings. For example, Barabas's asides remind Abigail how to find his hidden gold even as he pretends to lament her faked conversion to Christianity, and he falsely encourages both of her suitors while his continual asides announce his evil purpose. Although the black comedy that characterizes these plays is achieved by different means, we should not be surprised that these works often arouse a similar reaction. The authors were, no doubt, familiar with each other's literary efforts, and they may well have shared somewhat similar views on politics and religion. Indeed, only a few years after completing The Jew of Malta, Marlowe was 'wrytinge in one chamber' with Kyd. Douglas Cole in 'The Comic Accomplice in Revenge Tragedy,' Renaissance Drama (1966), 9:126, examines the problem of integrating the often comic effects associated with the tool villain with the tragic action of the plot. He finds that comedy in this genre tends 'to move from parody to satire, from a confrontation with style and method to a confrontation with human weakness, folly, and vice.'

my lips./ What an eye she casts on me! it twinkles like a star.' While he blackmails Barabas at her urging, Bellamira and her punk, Pilia-Borzia, encourage Ithamore to reveal still more ways to practice extortion on the Jew. Pilia-Borzia delivers Ithamore's demands for cash while the foul, bedraggled slave recites amorous couplets to a drab with many years of experience at her trade: 'Thou in those groves, by Dis above,/ Shall live with me and be my love.' His incorrect location for the god of the under-world and the incorporation of a line from one of Marlowe's purest love lyrics help make the scene a mockery of a passionate encounter. Ithamore is simultaneously comic, repulsive, and pathetic.

Even more important, the action in this play shows that underlings and tool villains are never content to remain in their station. Human nature being what it is, self-interest ultimately transforms all tool villains into would-be Machiavels. Except for the innocent Abigail, every character in The Jew of Malta is motivated by a concern for his advantage. Financial gain is the spur to action for Christian as well as Turk, and, as in the slave market, 'Every one's price is written on his back.' Peace is made 'but in hope of gold,' and treatises are broken to keep it:

> What wind drives you thus into Malta road?
> The wind that bloweth all the world besides,
> Desire of gold. (III.v.2–4)

In this world of Machiavels and Machiavels manqués, justice is not to be expected. In The Spanish Tragedy truth is ultimately revealed and the guilty are finally punished: 'Ay, heaven will be reveng'd of every ill.' But such a moral conclusion does not occur in The Jew of Malta. Here, the closing lines are especially sardonic: 'So, march away, and let due praise be given/ Neither to fate nor fortune, but to heaven.' These words, ironically claim-ing that heavenly righteousness has protected the citizens of Malta, are spoken by the Christian governor who twice broke his oath to the Turks, and who, by double-crossing Barabas, finally succeeds in regaining con-trol of the island. Heaven had nothing to do with this victory. The praise of heaven is bitterly comic, for the truth of the matter is that Ferneze, the governor, is really only a more clever Machiavel than his enemies. Events are ultimately determined not by a moral power in the universe but rather by the cunning of the most ruthless.

Shakespeare's Richard III, written shortly after Marlowe's play, demon-strates even more striking advances in the presentation of the tool villain and in the integration of the plotting.[13] The Duke of Buckingham, who is remarkably effective in aiding Richard's progress to the crown, is a figure of considerably more complexity than any earlier treatment of this type

---

[13] Emrys Jones in The Origins of Shakespeare, p. 200ff., points out other ways in which Kyd's Spanish Tragedy and Marlowe's Jew of Malta may have influenced Shakespeare's Richard III.

character in Renaissance drama. Moreover, his impact on the play is enhanced, for the activities of the tool villain are more closely integrated into the shape and movement of the action.

As Duke of Gloucester, Richard is derived not only from the Senecan hero of Renaissance tragedy and 'the formal Vice, Iniquity,' but also from the Machiavellian villain. He brags that he would even improve upon the advice of the Florentine and 'set the murderous Machiavel to school.' And being a Machiavel *par excellence*, Richard naturally makes use of a tool villain; for this purpose he cultivates Buckingham, a clever and ambitious assistant, who helps Gloucester seize the throne.

Buckingham enters the action only after Richard's personality, intentions, and cleverness have been clearly established. Shakespeare, in the same scene in which he first introduces Buckingham, manages to foreshadow his downfall in the curses and predictions of Queen Margaret:

> O Buckingham, take heed of yonder dog!
> Look when he fawns, he bites; and when he bites
> His venom tooth will rankle to the death.
> Have not to do with him; beware of him;
> Sin, death, and hell have set their marks on him,
> And all their ministers attend on him.
> ...
> What, dost thou scorn me for my gentle counsel,
> And soothe the devil that I warn thee from?
> O but remember this another day
> When he shall split thy very heart with sorrow,
> And say, poor Margaret was a prophetess.   (I.iii.289ff.)

At the close of the scene, Richard reveals in soliloquy that he is making allies of Buckingham and others by falsely blaming Queen Elizabeth and her family for the quarrel between his two brothers, King Edward IV and George, Duke of Clarence.

Margaret's anticipation of the tool villain's unhappy fate is restated with greater dramatic irony when, at his next appearance, Buckingham himself swears loving friendship to Elizabeth, her children, and supporters:

> Whenever Buckingham doth turn his hate
> Upon your Grace, [nor] with all duteous love
> Doth cherish you and yours, God punish me
> With hate in those where I expect most love.
> When I have most need to employ a friend,
> And most assured that he is a friend,
> Deep, hollow, treacherous, and full of guile
> Be he unto me: this do I beg of God,
> When I am cold in love to you or yours.   (II.i.32–40)

To emphasize the growing alliance between Richard and Buckingham, this scene closes as Richard repeats his slurs on the Queen's family, blaming them now for Clarence's death. Buckingham, accompanying Richard, exits with the ominous line, 'We wait upon your Grace.'

The transformation of Buckingham from a seemingly impartial courtier to a completely devoted agent of Richard has now begun. As his first real effort on Richard's behalf, Buckingham succeeds in convincing the Queen's allies that to ensure peace among all the factions, the young Prince Edward should be escorted into London for his coronation with only a small train of nobility – a plan that can easily be made to work to the advantage of the two schemers. At this early stage in their relationship, Buckingham obviously thinks of himself as Gloucester's political advisor, not simply as his agent: 'My lord, whoever journeys to the Prince,/ For God's sake let not us two stay at home,' he reminds Richard. The conspirators had agreed in some off-stage conference – 'the story we late talk'd of' – to separate the heir apparent from his mother's kindred. Richard responds to Buckingham's reminder of their plan with flattering high praise:

> My other self, my counsel's consistory,
> My oracle, my prophet, my dear cousin:
> I, as a child, will go by thy direction.   (II.ii.151–153)

In his customary manner, Gloucester presents himself as 'a plain man,' a naif, as one 'too childish-foolish for this world' who must put himself into the hands of Buckingham, wiser and more clever, one who can more capably protect Gloucester's own best interests.

To clarify the relationship between the Machiavel and his tool villain, to demonstrate how Richard uses Buckingham to dispossess Edward's heirs, Shakespeare deliberately alters his source and makes Buckingham appear to be the moving spirit for accompanying the prince with but a few members of the court. But, in fact, such a course of action would have been taken by Richard even without Buckingham's prompting; Buckingham is merely being allowed to think himself indispensable and wise. He is encouraged by Richard's flattery to hold an exaggeratedly high opinion of his usefulness and importance. In contrast, Shakespeare's source, Holinshed, adopting Sir Thomas More's account of the reign of Edward V and Richard III, actually gives Richard himself credit for arranging matters to his liking: he 'secretly by diverse means caused the Queen to be persuaded and brought to mind that neither were need and also should be jeopardous, the King [i.e. Prince Edward] to come up strong.'[14]

From this point in the play, Richard and Buckingham are closely allied in their actions, and events are being directed 'For the instalment of this noble Duke [of Gloucester]/ In the seat royal of this famous isle.' Rivers, Grey, and Vaughan are first imprisoned and then executed by order of 'the two mighty Dukes'; Prince Edward is lodged in the Tower with his younger brother, the Duke of York, taken out of sanctuary despite the efforts of their mother; and the conspirators hold their private counsels to promote the coronation of Richard while others meet to arrange the

---

[14] P. 124, 1587 ed.

crowning of Edward. For all his efforts on Richard's behalf, Buckingham is promised the earldom of Hereford.

Buckingham and Richard next engage in two theatrical performances. First, before the Lord Mayor, they appear costumed 'in rotten armor,' as though they had dressed hastily in the only defensive suits at hand. They claim that Hastings (who, in fact, had refused to support Richard as king) intended to rise against them, killing them both; in self-defense they had no choice but to defeat and imprison him. Now, however, Hastings' confession is regrettably unavailable since zealous friends have carried out his death sentence forthwith – still, 'the extreme peril of the cause' excuses their rashness. Next, after implying the illegitimacy not only of the two princes but even of the former King in order to strengthen Richard's own claim to the throne, Buckingham leads the Lord Mayor to a second interview with Richard. As they had agreed in casting their roles, Buckingham pleads with Richard to accept the crown and Richard follows Buckingham's instructions: 'still answer nay, and take it.' To set the scene they have staged with the right air of sanctimony, Richard appears with prayer-book in hand between two priests.

Shortly after this scene, Shakespeare alters his source once more so that the climactic act of the play, the murder of the princes in the Tower, becomes the cause of the break between the Machiavel and his tool villain. Richard asks Buckingham for his 'consent' to the murder, although his approval is hardly necessary. When it is not immediately forthcoming, Richard 'gnaws his lip' in anger. Buckingham's hesitation conveys the sense that these deaths are different from all those that have preceded them. In this instance, the victims are completely innocent; and, more important, they are the heaven-appointed successors to the throne. Before agreeing to an act so terrible, Buckingham now claims from Richard payment for his past assistance, the promised earldom of Hereford; Richard had told Buckingham he could 'look to have it yielded with all kindness.'

But Buckingham's reluctance is cause enough for Richard to turn on him: 'The deep-revolving, witty Buckingham/ No more shall be the neighbour to my counsels.' After all, Richard now has the crown and almost everything he desires. He has little further need of Buckingham, who, once paid, would prove of less usefulness and who might eventually become discontented, thinking himself insufficiently recompensed. Unlike Richard, Buckingham has nothing; he has, after all, received only the promise of reward. In his anger, Richard decides not only to discard Buckingham but also to deny his request for the earldom: 'I am not in the giving vein today.'

Having so quickly lost the new king's favor, Buckingham is wise enough to flee the court. His ensuing actions are reported to Richard: first, his revolt by joining the pro-Richmond faction; next, his ill-fortune, for his army is dispersed by sudden floods; and, finally, his capture. As he is led to the block, Buckingham recalls both his former oaths of allegiance to Edward IV, vows he so quickly broke, and the earlier curses of Queen

Margaret, which now 'fall heavy on my neck.'[15] In this way, his first appearance in the play and his execution are linked, for his life and fate form a carefully shaped and coherent design. Unlike the earlier examples we considered, the entire career of the tool villain here conforms to a well-organized pattern arranged by cause and effect, prediction and fulfillment.

Buckingham as tool villain functions neither as a dependent creature of the Machiavel like Pedringano nor as a quasi-distinct entity like Ithamore. Moreover, the irony of the tool villain's self-blindness is compounded in *Richard III*. Although this tool villain has greater self-awareness than his predecessors, greater intelligence and experience, Buckingham has gradually become assimilated by Richard, becoming Richard's instrument almost without realizing it – a fact that attests to Richard's own cleverness. Richard allows Buckingham to think that he is the cleverer politician who must guide his pupil on the surest road to the crown. Buckingham, after all, casts Richard in the role of devout: 'And look you get a prayer-book in your hand,/ And stand between two churchmen, good my lord:/ For on that ground I'll build a holy descant.' Only after the coronation does Richard reveal his unwillingness to manipulate Buckingham any longer, and only over the murder of the princes does Buckingham hesitate. In this way the killing of the princes becomes the turning point both for the relationship of Richard and Buckingham and for the play itself – another example of the superior plotting.

Indeed, compared with earlier dramas of the Machiavel and his tool villain, *Richard III* offers not only more complex characterizations and a broader canvas but also more intricate and pervasive dramatic irony. Throughout this play word and deed contradict one another so that one has a sense of the rightness of events as they occur; the dramatic irony unifies the action and reinforces the tone. The evidence of an ironic causality in the working out of the plot is demonstrated everywhere, leaving the spectator satisfied with the feeling that a kind of justice resides in the very grain of things, ultimately restoring the balance of good and evil. Appropriately the last of Richard's spectral visitors on the night before the battle of Bosworth Fields, Buckingham's ghost declares: 'The first was I that help'd thee to the crown;/ The last was I that felt thy tyranny./ O, in the battle think on Buckingham,/ And die in terror of thy guiltiness.' The wheel has come full circle, ending with curses and death; in their beginnings is their end. More complex than the relationship of Pedringano and Lorenzo and more coherent than the association of Ithamore and Barabas, the tool villain and the Machiavel in *Richard III* are intimately bound in an action that through lies, murder, and betrayal moves from trust to suspicion, from anger to hatred, and from revenge to death.

---

[15] Buckingham's speech is clearly in the style of *A Mirror for Magistrates* where his ghost expresses sorrow for past deeds and describes the punishments that befall sinners.

In the course of his career, Shakespeare created many versions of the tool villain. In *Hamlet*, the resourceful King Claudius co-opts Laertes into his instrument, turning one son who seeks to revenge the murder of his father against another. In this way, the behavior of the two young men is sharply contrasted at the same time as the cleverness of the usurper is demonstrated. Claudius's credentials as a Machiavel are further shown by his manipulating Rosencrantz and Guildenstern into tool villains who do his bidding. And in this way the true friendship of the Prince's classmate, Horatio, whom Hamlet will wear 'In my heart's core, ay, in my heart of heart,' may be contrasted with the false friendship of his two other school-fellows. Hamlet is quite right to trust them 'as adders fang'd'; at their deaths he feels no remorse, for 'they did make love to this employment.' In *King Lear*, Oswald as Goneril's tool villain has become cross-bred with the morality figure of the evil servant, and in this capacity he is defeated by the honest and loyal servant, Kent.[16] In *Othello*, the love-sick Roderigo is as much a simpleton or gull, duped by Iago, as he is the Machiavel's tool villain. Iago realizes correctly that Roderigo is both too foolish and too passive to serve as a useful agent. Indeed, his one real commission, to slay Cassio, is so badly bungled that Roderigo dies and his victim is only wounded. And *Pericles* presents two characters who would be tool villains but for the intervention of fate. The first of these, Thaliard, a minister at the court of the incestuous King of Antioch, is given poison and gold to murder the hero, but Pericles has wisely left his own kingdom for a period of sea travel. Leonine, the second tool villain in the play, is hired by the wicked Queen Dionyza to slay Marina, Pericles' daughter. But he is pre-vented when pirates suddenly appear and carry her off. Although not a man of strong compunction, Thaliard to his credit well understands the dangers of playing the role of tool villain:

> Here must I kill King Pericles; and if I do it not, I am sure to be hang'd at home; 'tis dangerous. Well, I perceive he was a wise fellow and had good discretion that, being bid to ask what he would of the king, desir'd he might know none of his secrets: now do I see he had some reason for't; for if a king bid a man be a villain, he's bound by the indenture of his oath to be one.
>
> (I.iii.1–8)

Not all courtiers would agree with Thaliard, however, as Shakespeare shows in a play written shortly after this.

The Winter's Tale offers perhaps the most interesting variant of the tool villain in the Shakespeare canon. In this work, the playwright, following his original source, presents a character who refuses to act the part of a murderous subordinate. Camillo, a trusted courtier, is ordered by King Leontes of Sicilia to poison Polixenes, King of Bohemia, a visiting friend,

---

[16] The evil servant, derived from the Morality character of the Vice, tends to initiate action and lead his master into the paths of temptation, whereas the tool villain serves to carry out the wicked intents of his employer. Such prodigal son plays as *Misogonus* (1570) and Gascoigne's *The Glass of Government* (1575) oppose good and evil servants.

since Leontes suspects Polixenes of seducing his Queen. At first rejecting Leontes' accusations and defending the honesty of the Queen, Camillo quickly comes to realize that irrational jealousy has possessed his ruler. Threatened by Leontes – 'Do't, and thou hast the one half of my heart; Do't not, thou splitt'st thine own' – Camillo says he will obey, though privately he determines to refuse:

> What case stand I in? I must be the poisoner
> Of good Polixenes, and my ground to do't
> Is the obedience to a master; one
> Who, in rebellion with himself, will have
> All that are his, so too. To do this deed,
> Promotion follows. If I could find example
> Of thousands that had struck anointed kings
> And flourish'd after, I'd not do't: but since
> Nor brass, nor stone, nor parchment bears not one,
> Let villainy itself forswear't. I must
> Forsake the court: to do't, or no, is certain
> To me a break-neck.   (I.ii.352–363)

Camillo warns Polixenes and leaves immediately with him for Bohemia.

After Leontes' madness has run its course, after the abandonment of his infant daughter, the warning of Apollo's oracle, and the death of his son, he comes to his senses. He realizes that Camillo, 'most humane/ And fill'd with honour,' acted morally: 'how he glisters/ Through my rust; and how his piety/ Does my deeds make the blacker!'

In the second half of the play, Camillo, having passed some sixteen years in Polixenes' court, finds that his wish to return to Sicilia can be combined with a desire to help the Prince of Bohemia and his shepherdess-sweetheart Perdita. In this way, Camillo becomes the agent for securing the happiness of the children of both Polixenes and Leontes, of restoring the lost Perdita to her parents, and of even gaining a wife for himself. He who would not be a tool villain proves instead to be an agent of a higher power, providential and beneficent, restoring beyond what reason might have thought possible that which was long lost and long lamented. This character, at least in comedies and romances, by refusing to play the part of a tool villain, can be an agent of love and reconciliation rather than of cruelty and death.

As these variations in the formula suggest, by the first decade of the seventeenth century, the straightforward and conventionalized dramatic figure of the Machiavel and the tool villain had become too familiar to be interesting. Repetition had made the terrors of the Machiavel only spectres to frighten babes, and the purely ironic ending was too customary to be effective. New combinations of personal qualities and new twists in the relationship of these characters were introduced to hold the audience's attention and to reflect the popular tastes of the time.

John Webster's *The Duchess of Malfi* presents what is surely one of the most powerful variations in the pattern of Machiavel, tool villain, and victim. For in this play, the Machiavellian instigators are motivated by forces that are both vaguely defined and terrifying. These include not simply position and wealth – 'I had a hope,/ Had she continu'd widow, to have gain'd/ An infinite mass of treasure by her death:/ And that was the main cause' – but also incest, lycanthropy, and a taste for cruelty of such intensity that its profound psychic sources remain forever hidden. The Machiavel is no longer one who simply desires political rule at any price; here the Cardinal is 'melancholy' and 'jealous' while his brother, Duke Ferdinand, is 'a most perverse and turbulent nature.' Together, they orchestrate the torment and the murder of their sister, the Duchess of Malfi.

Just as these Machiavels have changed, so, too, the tool villain has become more complex. Bosola, who had served the Cardinal some years earlier, receives gold from Ferdinand to act as his spy in the household of the Duchess. Bosola is not simply after reward or advancement; rather, he is disgusted by the corruption he sees everywhere around him, and he accepts the employment of the Duchess's brothers as proof that things are indeed as bad as he thought. He can feed the bitterness of his spirit by serving those he detests in an occupation he holds in contempt:' – what's my place?/ The provisorship o'th'horse? say then, my corruption/ Grew out of horse-dung: I am your creature.' In this way he can find confirmation on all sides that he is right in his opinion of most men and their morals. By his commentary and his extensive involvement in the action – Bosola appears in all five acts – what was usually a secondary or minor figure in the drama now controls the moral tone of the play. Indeed, Bosola becomes so independent that after serving as the tool villain and overseeing the execution of the Duchess, he becomes, in what is truly an extraordinary role reversal, her self-appointed revenger. The tool villain has now become a malcontent who turns out to be the revenger of his own victim. One might reasonably argue, in fact, that Bosola is the main character of this work, for, despite its title, the drama really focuses on him and on his growth and change. The play is, then, a psychological character study, tracing the effect on Bosola of his involvement with the Duchess and her second husband, Antonio.

Early in the action through the comments of those in her court, Webster establishes the Duchess as a strong-willed woman of spirit and integrity, admirable and chaste:

> Her days are practis'd in such noble virtue
> That sure her nights – nay more, her very sleeps –
> Are more in heaven than other ladies' shrifts.   (I.i.201–203)

But Bosola, rather weak-willed and skeptical of finding goodness in anyone, does not immediately share their estimate of her character. In time, he actually grows suspicious of her morals since ''Tis rumour'd she hath had three bastards, but/ By whom, we may go read i'th'stars.'

To protect Antonio, whom she has secretly married, from her brothers, the Duchess accuses him of dealing falsely with her accounts and dismisses him as her Master of the Household; he leaves for Ancona where they plan their reunion. Now at the midpoint of the play, Bosola expresses his real approval first for Antonio and then for the woman he has married. In opposition to the slanders invented against Antonio by those who were formerly his flatterers and unaware that he is actually her husband, Bosola praises the former Master of the Household when he shows the Duchess:

> what a most unvalu'd jewel
> You have, in a wanton humour, thrown away,
> To bless the man shall find him he was an excellent
> Courtier, and most faithful, a soldier that thought it
> As beastly to know his own value too little
> As devilish to acknowledge it too much:
> Both his virtue and form deserv'd a far better fortune.
>
> (III.ii.248–254)

Naturally, Bosola takes Antonio's mistreatment as another example that in this corrupt world virtue always goes unrewarded. Hearing her spouse so warmly praised, the Duchess reveals the true nature of her relationship with Antonio to Bosola, who responds with disbelief and congratulations:

> Duch: This good one that you speak of, is my husband.
> Bos:　Do I not dream? can this ambitious age
> 　　　Have so much goodness in't, as to prefer
> 　　　A man merely for worth, without these shadows
> 　　　Of wealth, and painted honours?　(III.ii.275–279)

But while he applauds their behavior for its moral soundness, Bosola, remaining true to his own position as 'intelligencer,' determines to send word to Ferdinand. In this way, so Bosola reasons, he will do as the world does, working for his own 'gain or commendation:/ Now, for this act I am certain to be rais'd.' Although he can appreciate and commend goodness and purity, Bosola takes what he finds to be the general corruption and self-interest of the world around him as an excuse to do what he himself knows to be wrong. Still, the battle lines are now drawn. Bosola progressively finds himself more and more torn between his hope of reward from her brothers and his growing admiration for the Duchess. Ultimately, he changes sides completely.

Soon arrested and imprisoned in her palace, the Duchess undergoes a series of shocking torments: she is presented with a severed hand, images of her dead family, and finally a masque performed by madmen to hideous music. By this torture, Ferdinand intends to punish his sister and 'bring her to despair.' Throughout, Bosola acts as his instrument while at the same time gradually developing an appreciation for the courage, dignity, and stoicism of his victim. He reports to Ferdinand that she conducts herself with 'a behaviour so noble/ As gives a majesty to adversity.'

According to Ferdinand, Bosola's feeling for the Duchess is unusual – 'Thy pity is nothing of kin to thee.' Yet even when Bosola feels compassion for her misery, the Duchess does not give way to self-pity:

> Thou art a fool then,
> To waste thy pity on a thing so wretch'd
> As cannot pity itself. (IV.i.88–90)

His admiration for her fortitude and his sympathy for her suffering result in Bosola's growing opposition to Ferdinand's orders:

> Faith, end here:
> And go no further in your cruelty –
> Send her a penitential garment to put on
> Next to her delicate skin, and furnish her
> With beads and prayer-books. (IV.i.116–120)

So moved by her anguish that he never wishes to see her again, Bosola is nevertheless forced by Ferdinand to return to the Duchess a last time. Ferdinand's insistence is surely sufficient to explain Bosola's presence in the scene that follows, but perhaps Bosola is also not a little curious to witness how the Duchess faces her own death and to discover whether her spirit and bravery remain with her to the end.[17]

After the masque performed by the insane, Bosola appears disguised as an old man. First he tells the Duchess he is her tomb-maker; her response is to 'be a little merry' on this subject. Then, with the entrance of her executioners, Bosola says he is

>   the common bellman
>   That usually is sent to condemn'd persons
>   The night before they suffer: –
> Duch: Even now thou said'st
>   Thou wast a tomb-maker.
> Bos: 'Twas to bring you
>   By degrees to mortification. (IV.ii.173–177)

The Duchess may be killed, but she will not be brought to fearful subjection or humiliation.[18] Unlike her maid Cariola, the Duchess will not protest, oppose, postpone, or fear her death:

> Duch: Who would be afraid on't?
>   Knowing to meet such excellent company
>   In th'other world.

---

[17] Una Ellis-Fermor in *The Jacobean Drama*, p. 178, describes him as a 'fitful, complex, and inconsistent plotter,' a 'reflective Machiavellian.'

[18] See Lisa Jardine, *Still Harping on Daughters*, p. 91, for a discussion of the Duchess's behaviour and the range of responses to it. 'Proved pathetically wrong in her belief in emancipation through hereditary strength, the Duchess is reduced to the safe composite stereotype of penitent whore, Virgin majestic in grief, serving mother, and patient and true turtle-dove mourning her one love. Strength of purpose is eroded into strength of character in adversity.'

Bos: Yet, methinks,
           The manner of your death should much afflict you,
           This chord should terrify you?
Duch: Not a whit:
           What would it pleasure me to have my throat cut
           With diamonds?   (IV.ii.209–217)

Ferdinand, tormented by guilt and madness, like other Machiavels, now rejects the tool villain he employed. Turned out without reward, Bosola finds himself 'like one/ That hath ta'en a sweet and golden dream:/ I am angry with myself, now I wake.' Having 'sought/ To appear a true servant, [rather] than an honest man,' Bosola, troubled by his 'guilty conscience,' by remorse and regret, by the realization 'that we cannot be suffer'd/ To do good when we have a mind to it!' actually gives way to tears of bitterness and dejection.

As a last resort, Bosola, frustrated, anguished, repentant, with a wild expression in his eyes, turns to the Cardinal for reward. The wily churchman, however, pretends to be ignorant of his sister's death and suggests that Bosola will find comfort at his hands only if he slays Antonio. Bosola feigns compliance:

> Well, I'll not freeze i'th'business;
> I would see that wretched thing, Antonio,
> Above all sights i'th'world.   (V.ii.143–145)

But his words are ambiguous. His strongly expressed wish to find Antonio does not explicitly state that he will kill him. Since he has learned from bitter experience that the Duchess's brothers are not trustworthy, Bosola, musing alone on stage, determines to test the Cardinal by using his mistress, Julia. Through her, Bosola discovers that both brothers indeed acted together to have the Duchess strangled – and for his part in this terrible crime, he has never been recompensed.

Over the body of Julia, whom he has just poisoned, the Cardinal once more promises Bosola that 'a fortune attends thee' with 'honours in store for thee' if he will murder Antonio. Once more, Bosola agrees, but when he is alone on stage he reveals his absolute determination to protect Antonio, for 'methinks the duchess/ Haunts me':

> I'll seek thee out, and all my care shall be
> To put thee into safety from the reach
> Of these most cruel biters, that have got
> Some of thy blood already. It may be
> I'll join with thee, in a most just revenge.   (V.ii.339–343)

But the tool villain, seeking his revenge, ironically kills tha man he most wishes to aid. Returning at night to the Cardinal's chamber to help remove Julia's body and discovering that his own death is planned, Bosola in the darkness mistakes Antonio for Ferdinand. Antonio had secretly entered the Cardinal's room thinking he could reconcile his brother-in-law with him by confronting the Churchman immediately after his prayers. On the line, 'Fall right my sword!' Bosola's weapon stabs the wrong man.

In the last scene of the play, the Machiavel and the tool villain have their final confrontation. The Cardinal, terrified of death, offers to 'divide/ Revenues.' But his proposition is, to use Bosola's word, 'unseasonable,' for the tool villain-turned-revenger is no longer tempted by gold. In the final resolution, Ferdinand, the Cardinal, and Bosola die, yet Bosola has come at last to realize that his participation in the brothers' cruelty was 'Much 'gainst mine own good nature' and his last act is to accomplish revenge for the agony and death of the Duchess of Malfi.

Even without considering its powerful, striking poetry and its intricate structure, whereby scenes and characters are carefully paralleled to dramatize similar and contrasting moments, *The Duchess of Malfi* is remarkable because it presents a character who begins as a tool villain but who develops in unusual ways. A man of bitter disappointments, a nihilist with a disregard for traditional morality, he is gradually transformed into a guilty creature, one who allows himself too late to admire the deep compassion, stoic courage, and unwavering dignity of a magnificent woman. At last realizing how his own sardonic turn of mind has distorted his view of life, he tries to correct his vision. Only the ironies of fortune prevent him from aiding anyone associated with the Duchess. Still, in the process of changing his outlook and allegiance, this tool villain has undergone a remarkable role change – from the agent of Machiavels to the revenger of their victim.

In *The Changeling*, Thomas Middleton and William Rowley give a new twist to both the character and the relationship of the tool villain and his employer. Indeed, the Machiavel who acquired the tool villain as an agent for his purposes has actually disappeared here. The devious practioner of *Realpolitik* who will stop at nothing in the pursuit of power and wealth has now given way to a new figure motivated by deeper, more individualized psychic and emotional forces. As we have already seen, Ferdinand, the Duchess of Malfi's cruel twin, is not driven simply by a desire for his sister's land or her money. Even more self-willed and obtuse in her behavior than Ferdinand, Beatrice-Joanna in *The Changeling* commissions the ill-favored villain DeFlores to murder her fiancé in order to free her to marry Alsemero, whom she finds more attractive. She has none of the political ambition of the Machiavel, nor does she, like the Machiavel, place herself above the moral order. Rather, she seems to believe only in a selective application of the moral code to her own actions. Moreover, her tool villain, who accepts a monetary down-payment and the promise of 'precious' reward, anticipates with special relish enjoying not the cash bonus – at one point Beatrice-Joanna offers to double her payment of 3,000 florins – but the love of the woman for whom he commits the murder:

You see I have thrown contempt upon your gold,
Not that I want it not, for I do piteously:
In order I will come unto't, and make use on't,
But 'twas not held so precious to begin with;
For I place wealth after the heels of pleasure,
And were I not resolv'd in my belief
That thy virginity were perfect in thee,
I should take my recompense with grudging,
As if I had but half my hopes I agreed for.   (III.iv.111–119)

The older, more business-like relationship between employer and agent has clearly metamorphosed into something quite different.

At the opening of the play, Beatrice-Joanna's dislike of DeFlores, her father's servant, is so intense that she herself recognizes it as irrational: ''tis my infirmity,/ Nor can I other reason render.' The very sight of him is distressing for her. Just as she finds him a 'thing most loath'd,' DeFlores, for his part, feels compelled to seek her out: as he explains, though 'I know she hates me,/ Yet cannot choose but love her.' How very different is this love-hate relationship from the straight-forward and clear-cut self-serving combination of Buckingham and Richard III. Yet, despite, their lack of self-control, the central figures in The Changeling are also well aware that they are being driven helplessly by forces beyond their own under-standing and direction. As DeFlores admits:

I can as well be hang'd as refrain seeing her;
Some twenty times a day, nay, not so little,
Do I force errands, frame ways and excuses
To come into her sight, and I have small reason for't,
And less encouragement; for she baits me still
Every time worse than other.   (II.i.28–33)

Although Beatrice-Joanna detests him, she initially turns to DeFlores for help on quite plausible grounds. Self-indulgent, pampered, and shallow, she has confused appearance for reality, mistaking beauty for goodness and ugliness for evil. On this basis, applying what she thinks is strict logic to her dilemma, she employs DeFlores – 'the ugliest creature/ Creation fram'd for some use' – to perform an ugly deed – the murder of her fiancé. She responds to DeFlores in the same way that she responds to Piracquo, to whom she is unhappily engaged. But were I a man, she says,

I should not then be forc'd to marry one
I hate beyond all depths, I should have power
Then to oppose my loathings, nay, remove 'em
For ever from my sight.   (II.ii.110–113)

Her words – 'hate,' 'loathings,' 'remove 'em/ For ever from my sight' – exactly describe her reaction to DeFlores and could be as easily applied to Piracquo. Whom better, then, could she choose to eliminate Piracquo? And what could be more reasonable than her plan of action: 'I shall rid myself/ Of two inveterate loathings at one time,/ Piracquo, and his dog-face [i.e. DeFlores].'

But logic cannot be applied to what is illogical, and her arguments can hardly convince DeFlores of the unreasonableness of his passion for her. Once Piracquo is dead, DeFlores is so determined to enjoy Beatrice-Joanna himself that he threatens to 'confess all' if she refuses him. His employment as her agent has made him her equal; 'nor,' according to him, 'is it fit we two, engag'd so jointly,/ Should part and live asunder.' Unshakeable in his absolute insistence that she yield herself to him, De-Flores forces Beatrice-Joanna to acknowledge her complicity in the murder and her dependence on his continued cooperation.

But unlike the earlier examples – Barabas blackmailed by Ithamore or Richard disappointed in Buckingham – Beatrice-Joanna does not attempt to eliminate DeFlores. Instead, the action takes an extraordinarily subtle turn, for its psychological validity is based on a phenomenon that social scientists have only recently identified. Experience has demonstrated that long-held hostages, dependent for their very existence on the good will of their kidnappers, soon come to protect, defend, and even identify with those who hold them captive. In the same way, Beatrice-Joanna, believing in a morality of appearances, comes to love DeFlores for the care with which he guards her reputation: 'I'm forc'd to love thee now,/ 'Cause thou provid'st so carefully for my honour.' When her maid returns dangerously late from the bridal chamber where she substituted her virginity in place of the bride's, Beatrice-Joanna finds that DeFlores is ready with a plan to eliminate the tardy and untrustworthy waiting woman. His efforts claim her devotion:

> How rare is that man's speed!
> How heartily he serves me! His face loathes one,
> But look upon his care, who would not love him?
> The east is not more beauteous than his service. (V.i.69–72)

And as she watches him directing affairs, she repeats her words of admiration: 'Here's a man worth loving,' 'a wondrous necessary man.'

With perfect irony, Beatrice-Joanna's guilt is revealed through her sudden intimacy with DeFlores. Her 'tender attachment' to him – 'He's now become your arm's supporter, your/ Lip's saint!' – is so radical a change in her behavior that it makes her new husband, Alsemero, seriously doubt her honesty, confirming the report of the dead maid about her mistress's conduct. Judging by her own muddled standard of morality, Beatrice-Joanna absolutely repudiates Alsemero's charge of 'adultery.' In her mind, he is giving way to 'false suspicion.' She tells him, 'Remember I am true unto your bed,' for she committed murder and adultery only to enable them to marry: 'having no/ Better means than that worst, to assure/ Yourself to me.' For this reason she believes herself innocent. Beatrice-Joanna tells Alsemero that since 'your love has made me/ A cruel murd'ress' and since sexual infidelity and murder, all 'for your sake was done,' then Alsemero is himself a party to these deeds, benefits from them, and shares in the responsibility for them. Her logic is especially ironic, for she had earlier prevented Alsemero from challenging Piracquo to a duel, an honorable if less predictable way to resolve the rivalry between the two men. Finally, since she has participated in these crimes only as a last resort and since she has done so unwillingly – 'I have kiss'd poison for't' – she has, at least in her own mind, maintained her own purity of action; she can exonerate herself: 'I stand up innocence.'

She responds to her husband's suspicions with complete assurance of her righteousness, for in Beatrice-Joanna's mind her guilt can actually prove her innocence:

> To your bed's scandal, I stand up innocence,
> Which even the guilt of one black other deed
> Will stand for proof of: your love has made me
> A cruel murd'ress. (V.iii.62–65)

Her confusion of moral values, her warped sense of right and wrong, finds perfect expression in the mangled ethics of her argument. When they had first appeared in English drama, the Machiavel and his agent understood conventional morality but rejected it; later Machiavels and their tool villains doubted, questioned, and tested the validity of conventional morality. Beatrice-Joanna, however, lacks any comprehension of a moral code until she is at the point of death. She achieves a moment of insight only when she is carried onstage dying, and only then does she seem to grasp the enormity of her sins or understand the extent of her crimes. Her last words to her father express something of this new sense of her self-loathing and self-disgust:

> Oh come not near me, sir; I shall defile you.
> I am that of your blood was taken from you
> For your better health; look no more upon't,
> But cast it to the ground regardlessly;
> Let the common sewer take it from distinction. (V.iii.149–153)

Her accomplice, on the other hand, has always realized the terrible price he was paying. Nevertheless, for DeFlores the love of Beatrice-Joanna is so 'sweet recompense' that all else is 'light and cheap.' He is absolute, fixed in his determination to enjoy her as the price for his conscience: 'Can you weep fate from its determin'd purpose?/ So soon may you weep me.'

> If I enjoy thee not, thou ne'er enjoy'st.
> I'll blast the hopes and joys of marriage,
> I'll confess all; my life I rate at nothing. (III.iv.147–149)

DeFlores has always been obsessed with her and his admiration never wavers:

> Yes, and her honour's prize
> Was my reward; I thank life for nothing
> But that pleasure: it was so sweet to me
> That I have drunk up all, left nothing behind
> For any man to pledge me. (V.iii.168–171)

Almost alone in the play, he has not proved a changeling in his affections. Unlike the fickle and shallow Beatrice-Joanna, DeFlores is a character of enormous strength of purpose and commitment, admirable in his heroic, if misguided, dedication to a woman unworthy of his devotion. In this instance, the tool villain is no longer the dupe of his employer. Here the secondary agent, the 'base second means' to use Hotspur's phrase, is not so much acted upon as acting, for he has been transformed into a clever shaper of the action, a manipulator of the plot. Love has replaced politics; the Machiavel has faded from view; and a new, confused, and peculiar moral vision affects the relationship of the tool villain and his employer.

As politics and political power became less valued, the Machiavel and the tool villain who served him disappeared in the drama; both of these type characters, as we have seen, became metamorphosed into more complex creations who could sustain more entangled relationships. But long after Middleton and Rowley, writers knew that devious, evil schemers would continue to make use of willing assistants to accomplish their dirty work. The generic Vice figure of the old Morality plays, after all, was simply carrying out the wishes of Satan whom he served, and the combination of villain and henchman remained well established long after the Renaissance. Even comic villainy prefers to achieve its effects through agents: Lady Sneerwell in Sheridan's *The School for Scandal* employs Snake as her instrument. And to cause the more serious suffering of the nineteenth century novel, we find that a character such as Compeyson, the maliciously cruel and wicked tormentor of Magwitch and Miss Havisham in Dickens' *Great Expectations*, takes the brutal Orlick as his tool. The motivation and means may have changed over time, but the combination of these two characters remains a constant.

VI

The Shrew

The shrew is a highly distinctive character in Renaissance drama; indeed, among female roles she is surely among the earliest, most popular, and most memorable.[1] Petruchio, the hero of Shakespeare's *The Taming of the Shrew*, remembers that Socrates' wife, Xantippe, was said to be 'curst and shrewd' (I.ii.), so Shakespeare and his contemporaries were clearly well acquainted with women of similar temperament if not from life then from legend. In literature, Chaucer's Wife of Bath was a well-known example, and the traditional characterization in medieval mysteries of Noah's wife as a stubborn, willful, and even violent harridan made her a popular favorite in dramatizations of the Flood.

Naturally, the shrew is a valuable stock figure for a writer, for she raises questions about the proper role of women. Her actions seem to focus attention on such issues as the extent of a woman's independence from her parents in the choice of a spouse and the extent of her freedom of action as a wife and mother. To consider the range of views about this figure held toward the close of Elizabeth's reign and during the first decade of James's rule, we shall examine three closely related plays, works similar in theme as well as story: the anonymous *The Taming of a Shrew* (1589), Shakespeare's *The Taming of the Shrew* (1594), and John Fletcher's sequel to Shakespeare's play, *The Woman's Prize, or The Tamer Tam'd* (1611).[2]

Three failings in particular mark a woman as a shrew: she is invariably talkative, combative, and assertive. According to Renaissance culture, these traits are feminine defects, for women were praised for their silence, admired for their modest and retiring manner, and taught to be obedient and subservient. Henry Parrot describes the behavior of the shrew in his amusing catch-all *VIII Cures for the Itch; Characters, Epigrams, and Epitaphs* (1626).

---

[1] M. C. Bradbrook calls the shrew 'the only native comic role for women.' 'Dramatic Role as Social Image, a study of *The Taming of the Shrew*,' *Shakespeare Jahrbuch* (1958), 132–150.
[2] These dates are listed in the Harbage-Schoenbaum *Annals of English Drama*.

Shees of all other creatures most untameablest, and covets more the last word in scoulding, then doth a Combater the last stroke for victorie. She lowdest lifts it [i.e. the last word] standing at her door, bidding with exclamation flat defiance to any one sayes blackes her eye. She dares appeare before any Justice, nor is least daunted with the sight of Counstable, nor at worst threatnings of a Cuckingstoole. There's nothing mads or moves her more to outrage, then but the very naming of a waspe, or if you sing or whistle when she is scoulding. If any in the interim chance to come within her reach, twenty to one she scratcheth him by the face: or doe but offer to hold her hands, sheel presently begin to cry out murder. ... Her manner is to talke much in her sleepe what wrongs she hath indured of that rogue her husband whose hap may be in time to dye a Martyr.[3]

Parrot's sketch highlights the typical shrew's faults of an uncontrolled tongue – 'worse than the biting of a Scorpion' – an argumentative nature, and a fierce temper, all of which make her a torment for her husband.

Indeed, writers of the time were by and large in agreement on the proper relationship of daughters to parents and wives to husbands, and the shrew's behavior explicitly contradicts the standard notions of acceptable female conduct. For example, it was thought that choosing a mate without parental advice and consent denied parents their responsibility for negotiating and approving a spouse, an approval that was essential when financial arrangements and dowries were important aspects of marriage. Although the personal feelings of the young people were to be taken into account, the Protestant clergy of the English Renaissance granted parents the ultimate authority for arranging marriages. In keeping with its lengthy title, John Stockwood's 1589 pamphlet contains evidence 'Shewing that children are not to marie, without the consent of their parentes, in whose power and choise it lieth to provide wives and husbandes for their sonnes and daughters.' Stockwood even believed that rebellious children were the evil that caused God to visit the plague on England as punishment! And, in agreement with Stockwood, the widely followed minister Henry Smith, whose *Preparative to Marriage* (1591) had three editions in the year of its publication, argued that children should marry those chosen by their parents.

In this same sermon, Smith, who 'always had an especially large attendance at his wedding sermons,'[4] also warns that an unhappy home is caused by those termagants who

overthwart, and upbraide, and sue the preheminence of their Husbands. ... As David exalteth the love of women above all other loves; so Salomon mounteth the envie of women above all other envies, stubborne, sullen, taunting, gainsaying, out-facing, with such a bitter humour, that one would thinke they were molten out of the salt pillar into which Loths wife was transformed. We say not, all are alike, but this sect hath manie Disciples. Dooth the ribbe that is in a mans side fret him, or gall him? no more should she which is made of the ribbe. Though a woman bee wise and painfull

---

[3] Parrot, n.p.
[4] Lu Emily Pearson, *Elizabethans at Home*, p. 294.

[painstaking], and have many good parts, yet if she bee a shrewe, her trouble-some jarring in the end will make her honest behaviour unpleasant as her over pinching at last causeth her good huswiferie to be evill spoken of. Therefore although she be a Wife, yet some time she must observe the servants lesson, Not answering againe, &c hold her peace to keep the peace. Therefore they which keepe silence, are well said to holde their peace, because silence oftentimes doth keep the peace, when wordes would breake it.

To her silence and patience she must adde the acceptable obedience, which makes a Woman rule while she is ruled. This is the Wives tribute to her Husband; for she is not called his head, but hee is called her head.[5]

As the shrew causes unhappiness in marriage, the good wife, according to Smith, creates marital bliss by understanding her husband's disposition and by making herself obedient to his will.

Surely the most orthodox statement of a wife's role in matrimony is to be found in the Homily 'The Sermon of the State of Matrimony.' Homilies, after all, present the official position of the Elizabethan Church on such subjects as salvation, fear of death, whoredom and adultery, and rebellion, and, 'except there be a sermon,' a homily from the Book of Homilies was ordered to be read in every parish church every Sunday. 'And when the foresaid booke of Homilies is read over, her Majesties pleasure is, that the same be repeated & read againe, in such sort as was before prescribed.' Although private opinions might vary according to the sectarian beliefs, class, or sex of the individual, the government's position, and therefore the Church's position, was unmistakable:

nowe as concerning the wives duetye. What shall become her? shall she abuse the gentlenesse and humanity of her husband; and, at her pleasure, turne all thinges upside down? No surely. For that is far repugnant against Gods commandement: For thus doth S. Peter preach to them, Ye wives, be ye in subjection to obey your own husbandes. To obey, is an other thing then to controle or command, which yet they may doe, to their children, and to their family: But as for their husbandes, them must they obey, and cease from commaunding, and performe subjection. For this surely doeth nourishe concorde very much, when the wife is readye at hande, at her husbandes commaundement, when shee will apply her selfe to his will, when she endevoureth her selfe to seeke his contentation, and to doe him pleasure, when shee will eschew all things that might offende him: For thus will most truely bee verified the saying of the Poet: A good wife by obeying her husbande, shall beare the rule, so that hee shall have a delight and a gladnes, the sooner at all times to returne home to her. ... As S. Paule expresseth it in his fourme of words, Let women be subject to their hus-bandes, as to the Lord: for the husband is the head of the woman, as Christ is the heade of the Church. Heere you understande, that God hath com-manded that ye should acknowledge the authority of the husband and referre to him the honour of obedience.[6]

---

[5] Pp. 82–84.
[6] The Second Tome of Homilies, 1587. No. 18, 'Of the State of Matrimony,' pp. 482–483.

Once again, women in marriage must learn obedience, practice sub-mission, and 'performe subjection.' The successful fulfillment of their role as wives is to be judged completely by the degree of happiness of their husbands.

The emphasis of the Protestant clergy on the desirability of a woman's subservience in marriage is clear enough. What is less clear to modern critics is how the prevailing religious teachings actually affected the role of women. On the one hand, some critics claim that, paradoxically, a woman gained greater independence. They argue that the increasing strength of the Puritans, whose party was growing in power, claimed 'the only justifi-cation for a wife's submission was a diplomatic one that mutual comfort – to them the chief end of marriage – required it.' From examining sermons and moral tracts published during the period 1558–1640, they have deter-mined 'it cannot be doubted that a gradual improvement in the position of women is discernible [especially] in the works treating of marriage and the home. ... The increased emphasis upon women's spiritual and material rights paved the way that led toward theoretical equality – a position a few writers in the early seventeenth century were already begin-ning to maintain.'[7] On the other hand, other critics claim that women were becoming far less independent than they had been, for Protestant-ism had contradictory and conflicting effects: 'with the coming of the Protestant ascendancy a new emphasis was placed upon the wife's duty and subjection to her husband. ... Pressures from Protestant clergymen strongly urged a return to the concept of docility in women and wives. Luther's view that women should mind the house and bring up the chil-dren was echoed and supported by Protestant theologians and lay per-sons throughout England.'[8] And 'in spite of the wider range of opportuni-ties which became available to (some) women during the Renaissance and Reformation, attitudes towards women did not perceptibly change – may in fact have become somewhat hardened as individual women chal-lenged traditional roles.'[9]

So wide a spectrum of interpretation suggests that widely differing views were actually held, some clearly more liberal than others. Such is indeed the case. To cite one instance, the popular Reverend Smith argued against wife-beating – 'Husbands must hold their hands and Wives their tungs' – but other clergymen recited the doggerel: 'A spaniel, a woman, and a walnut tree,/ The more they are beaten, the better they be.'[10] In addition, we must remember that the sermons and conduct manuals by which we now attempt to evaluate the role and the rights of Renaissance women do not set out to reflect life, but rather intend to establish the standards by which it should be lived. Drama, in contrast, tends to mirror the reality of social mores more closely.

---

7 Louis B. Wright, *Middle-Class Culture in Elizabethan England*, pp. 226–227.
8 Marjorie Garber, *The Coming of Age in Shakespeare*, p. 124.
9 Lisa Jardine, *Still Harping on Daughters*, p. 58.
10 Pearson, p. 375.

Naturally, the accuracy of drama as an imitation of life depends on the artistry and attitudes of the dramatist. As we shall see, a comparison of our closely related shrew-taming plays will reveal that each presents a very different notion of the proper behavior for women and of the joys of marriage.

We may begin with the simplest, and, perhaps, the earliest of the three, for several scholars postulate that the anonymous *The Taming of a Shrew* was derived from a no longer extent Shakespearean play which, in revised form, was published in the 1623 Folio. In any case, whatever its relationship to Shakespeare's work, most critics agree that *A Shrew* belongs to 'rather a different type from the bad quartos of other Shakespearean plays.'[11] According to Richard Hosley, *The Taming of a Shrew* 'involves a good deal more conscious originality on the part of its author or authors than is usually to be observed in bad-quarto texts.'[12] Indeed, the presentation of the shrew character in this work provides in no small measure a gauge to the difference in attitude between Shakespeare and his imitators.

An important distinguishing quality of *A Shrew* is that the motivation of Kate as well as of most of the other characters is usually made so explicit, so limited, that their behavior seems crude and oversimplified. For example, Kate has a soliloquy bluntly stating her feelings:

> But yet I will consent and marrie him,
> For I methinkes have livde too long a maid,
> And match him too, or else his manhoods good.   (v.40–43)

Although she explains that she is bored with the role of daughter and will compete with her new husband for dominance, the play never presents any hint why Kate feels this way. Neither the action nor the dialogue offers any real insight into Kate's nature: why she is discontented in her father's household; why she is determined to test, challenge, or threaten her fiancé's masculinity. In effect, what the text gains in explicitness, it loses in richness and implication. Her lines fail to suggest that Kate actually feels attracted to her suitor.

Kate's failure to reveal any feelings of tenderness toward her husband until the end of *A Shrew* is in keeping with her restricted range of emotions. Her temperament is limited to manifestations of willfulness and anger at the start and to subservience and submissiveness at the close. This shrew continues to refuse food even when starved:

> Ile nere be beholding to you for your Meate,
> I tell thee flatlie here unto the thy teethe
> Thou shalt not keepe me nor feede me as thou list,
> For I will home againe unto my fathers house.   (xi.39–42)

---

[11] Brian Morris, the Arden edition, p. 32.
[12] 'Sources and Analogues of *The Taming of The Shrew*,' HLQ, (1963–64), pp. 289–308.

And the husband holds out until his wife has been reformed into a woman 'meeke and gentell.'

The shrew-tamer's methods and goals present the conservative school of thought on the appropriate treatment of women and their proper place in marriage. For example, the shrew-tamer's success is demonstrated when he has thoroughly brow-beaten his wife; with no will of her own, her responses can only be in total agreement with her now-contented spouse: 'why thus must we two live,/ One minde, one heart, and one content for both.' These newlyweds have little sense of mutual enjoyment.

The view of marriage that best pleases her husband is most fully expounded in Katherine's last speech, explaining 'what dutie wives doo owe unto their husbands.' For her argument Katherine basis her assessment of the character of women on an interpretation of *Genesis*. According to her reading, the *Bible* tells us that woman is 'the woe of man ... for that, by her came sinne to us,/ And for her sine was *Adam* doomd to die.' Women as the source of sin and death, the curse of mankind, are surely beings very inferior to their partners. By referring to the absolute, divinely ordained hierarchy that ordered 'all things to stand in perfit course,' Katherine concludes that women's place is beneath men's, for they are inferior both morally and intellectually. Then by her actions she proceeds to demonstrate this inferior status quite literally:

> As Sara to her husband, so should we,
> Obey them, love them, keepe, and nourish them,
> If they by any meanes doo want our helpes,
> Laying our handes under theire feete to tread,
> If that by that we, might procure there ease,
> And for a president Ile first begin,
> And lay my hand under my husbands feete. (xviii.37–43)

From the events in the play we should conclude that the qualities most necessary for a happy marriage are submission and subordination by wives – to the extent of risking their fingers! – as well as dominance and aggressive persistence by husbands. This attitude, making the husband the absolute ruler of the household, was, after all, in keeping with one strain of Protestant thought on the subordination of women to male authority. As William Perkins explains, 'A couple is that whereby two persons standing in mutual relation to each other are combined together, as it were into one. And of these two the one is always higher and beareth rule; the other lower and yieldeth subjection.' [13] This is the position supported by the action and dialogue in *The Taming of a Shrew*, by the shrew-tamer's behavior, and by Kate's description of woman as 'the woe of man.'

---

[13] *Works*, pp. 418–419.

Shakespeare's *The Taming of the Shrew* portrays far more distinctive and complex figures than we found in *A Shrew*, as a comparison of parallel scenes clearly reveals. Here the shrew, because she matures through her experiences, arrives at an entirely different understanding of the nature of happiness in marriage. At the opening of the play we discover that not all men can exercise male authority: Baptista Minola, for example, is hardly one to attempt to impose his judgment on either Katherine or her younger sister, Bianca, for he is totally unsuccessful at getting his daughters to do anything they do not want to do. They, in turn, know that eventually they can have their way either by outright resistance or by a pretense of obedience. Katherine and Bianca intend to marry only men of their own choosing. At the opening of Act II, Katherine tries to force Bianca into confessing which of her suitors she really loves. The dialogue here, still early in the action of the play, reveals that the sisters fully expect to follow their own inclinations:

> Kath: Is't not Hortensio?
> Bian: If you affect him, sister, here I swear
> I'll plead for you myself but you shall have him.
> Kath: O then belike you fancy riches more.
> You will have Gremio to keep you fair.
> Bian: Is it him you do envy me so?
> Nay then you jest, and now I well perceive
> You have but jested with me all this while.   (II.i.13–20)

Moreover, both of them look forward to marriage. Bianca with her demure and alluring manner has already attracted suitors by her 'beauteous modesty,' and Katherine, resentful of the popularity and reputation of her sister, fears she will be left an old maid. She complains to her father of the preferential treatment Bianca seems to receive:

> Nay, now I see
> She is your treasure, she must have a husband,
> I must dance barefoot on her wedding-day,
> And for your love to her lead apes in hell.
> Talk not to me, I will go sit and weep.   (II.i.31–35)

Katherine longs to marry despite her evident desire to have the upper hand in all affairs; she is, no doubt, well aware that in Renaissance England the choices in occupation and life style for respectable unmarried women were severely restricted. Nevertheless, one might well have expected Katherine to be somewhat less interested in acquiring suitors and less eager to become a wife. In fact, Katherine seems to be revealing indirectly that she accepts, at least in part, some of the norms of her society, even though she appears determined not to conform outwardly to those norms. Clearly, her rebellion against social conventions, her refusal to act according to the role expected for proper womanly conduct is neither absolute nor thorough.

For their part, her father and her prospective husband have no intention of forcing Katherine into a wedding against her will. Baptista tells

Petruchio that Katherine's love is the essential element to any marriage agreement; the arrangements for dowry and union can be signed only after Petruchio has succeeded in winning her: 'when the special thing is well obtain'd,/ That is, her love; for that is all in all.' Petruchio, too, realizes that he must direct his confident and forceful style of courtship to one essential aim: Baptista will grant him no bride and no dowry unless 'I get your daughter's love.' The discussion between the two men simply establishes Petruchio's eligibility as son-in-law and the terms of the dowry. But proceeding any further depends entirely on Katherine's reaction to her untraditional suitor from Verona.

After a reminder of how great a challenge dealing with Katherine can be – she has just broken Hortensio's lute over his head – we witness the first meeting of shrew and shrew-tamer. But first Petruchio announces in soliloquy that he will imitate Katherine, exceeding her in contrariness. Actually, the word 'shrew' is etymologically sexless; and, indeed, Petruchio will prove as great a shrew as Katherine. There is method to his madness: as his servant recognizes, Petruchio's treatment of Kate is designed to 'kill her in her own humour.' Now she is to discover how well-suited Petruchio is as a prospective husband. He is as imaginative and quick-witted, as contrary and obstinate, and almost as physical and forceful as the woman he woos: when she strikes him, he threatens to strike her back. Still, when her father appears, she naturally criticizes his choice of a suitor and refuses the offer of a speedy wedding: 'I'll see thee hang'd on Sunday first.' Yet we should notice that at no time does Katherine actually refuse to wed Petruchio. As is to be expected, she finds fault with him; and, of course, she thinks the coming Sunday too soon for adequate preparation. But she never rejects him as bridegroom and, in fact, silently joins hands with him in a ceremony that seems to approach the binding pre-contract commitment of an Elizabethan marriage.[14]

> Bap: I know not what to say, but give me your hands.
> God send you joy, Petruchio, 'tis a match.
>
> Gre ⎱
> Tra ⎰ : Amen say we. We will be witnesses.
>
> (II.i.311–31)

Possibly Kate now even kisses Petruchio as he asks, and, at least according to the stage directions in the First Folio, they leave the stage together, not 'separately' as in later versions.[15] We notice from their very first quarrel that when they spar, their spirited interchange demonstrates that they are well-suited; their lively war of words ends with a kiss, a token of love,

---

[14] George Hibbard, introduction to the New Penguin Edition.

[15] The addition to the stage direction that has Katherine and Petruchio go off in different directions rather than together, made originally by Theobald, is a good example of how easily this play may be altered in crucial ways by minor changes in staging and acting. Perhaps more than any other early comedy, The Taming of The Shrew can be made to accomodate widely differing interpretations by the most modest of means. See Irene G. Dash, Wooing, Wedding, and Power, for an interesting discussion of the stage history of the play.

however reluctantly given. In fact, Katherine kisses Petruchio three times during the action of Shakespeare's play, and with each kiss the intensity of their mutual affection is made progressively more evident. In contrast, the Petruchio character in *A Shrew* justly complains, 'I . . . never get a kisse.'

Katherine and Petruchio next meet on their wedding day. His tardiness prompts Katherine to complain of her future husband and repeat that she is reluctant to marry him, 'forc'd/ To give my hand, oppos'd against my heart,/ Unto a mad-brain rudesby.' Yet for all her reluctance, she is angry that he is late and fears he may not appear at all. If she would really prefer not to marry him, she would not weep but, on the contrary, be delighted by his absence. And most inconsistent of all for a woman who flouts conventional behavior, Katherine is mortified that people will know she has been jilted if her fiancé fails to appear: 'Now must the world point at poor Katherine,/ And say 'Lo, there is mad Petruchio's wife, If it would please him come and marry her.'' In the back of her mind she must know why a man might have second thoughts about making her his wife. She leaves the stage in tears. Katherine obviously is not indifferent to public opinion, no matter how strenuously her conduct may defy the behavior code of the day. She is very different from the heroine of *A Shrew*, who never worries about public opinion, never expresses concern for her reputation, and never cries.

Defying the code of behavior is not unique to Katherine. Since she often acts unconventionally, Petruchio demonstrates how two can play that game. When he finally arrives for his wedding, dressed in an outrageous costume and with a lackey who is 'a very monster in apparel,' he proceeds to swear in church, strike the priest, and throw 'sops all in the sexton's face.'

Once again report confirms how well-matched in temperament are the bride and groom, for Petruchio is described as 'a devil, a devil, a very fiend,' and his wife as 'a devil, a devil, the devil's dam.' The groom realizes that the basis for a happy life with his new bride can be established only if the newlyweds promptly leave the society that Katherine has dominated in the past. A new comportment should accompany her new position as a married woman, but a new mode of conduct can be learned only if she is removed from her submissive father. She cannot now be allowed to re-sume her old behavior patterns or Petruchio will lose all chance of helping her grow into a loving spouse. Moreover, if her husband hopes to have any authority in his household, he must assert himself forthwith. Petruchio achieves his ends first by insisting that they depart at once – as he says to his friends, shocked by his hastiness, 'If you knew my business,/ You would entreat me rather go than stay' – and then by ordering Katherine to leave with him. She is 'rescued' against her own wish to remain and enjoy the bridal feast.

Operating on the theory that we can soonest recognize our faults not in ourselves but in others, Petruchio, once in his own home, mimics Katherine's behavior. He becomes impatient, hasty, quarrelsome, violent, impossible-to-please. Unlike the heroine of *A Shrew*, who is too obtuse to sympathize with the servants when her husband beats them and who never seems to realize that his treatment of them is an implied threat to her, Shakespeare's heroine begs Petruchio to have 'patience' and prays that he 'be not so disquiet.' As one of his servants realizes, 'he is more shrew than she,' for Petruchio also reasons logically that it takes a shrew to tame a shrew. And Katherine, cast in a new role as wife to a shrewish husband, now tries to calm his temper as others earlier had tried to cool her fury. He 'rails, and swears, and rates' to 'kill her in her own humour' so that Katherine can adopt a new self-image. And her reformation cannot be far off: for the moment she 'sits as one new risen from a dream.'[16]

In soliloquy, Petruchio points out that he is modeling his treatment of Katherine along the lines set down for taming a wild bird – keeping her hungry, exhausted, and carefully watched. He will maintain her in this state of anxiety by his own absurd action – 'Some undeserved fault/ I'll find about the making of the bed' – and by his deliberately frenzied zaniness: 'heere I'll fling the pillow, there the bolster,/This way the coverlet, another way the sheets.'

All is plotted so that he will 'with the clamor keep her still awake' and by his own madness 'curb her mad and headstrong humour.' He will 'rail and brawl' like any shrew. And 'amid this hurly I intend/ That all is done in reverend care of her.' Petruchio will demonstrate that he can play Kate's game. Wittily congratulating himself on his cleverness, he even addresses the audience directly, challenging his listeners to improve on his tactics: 'He that knows better how to tame a shrew,/ Now let him speak; 'tis charity to show.' He is proving not that he is physically stronger, but that he is her equal in shrewishness, a shrewishness that ostensibly has her interest at heart. He intends to reform her by his 'considerate' behavior – thus he will 'kill a wife with kindness.' Indeed, Katherine realizes at her next entrance that whatever he does, 'He does it under name of perfect love' – which, of course, makes his conduct even more infuriating. As he explains, all his extensive efforts are carried on for her benefit.

No Elizabethan familiar with the theory of bird-training would doubt Petruchio's success. This is a conditioning process that even the shrew-tamer of A Shrew recalled, though he applied its principles in rather brutal fashion. The husband of A Shrew offers none of Petruchio's wonderful irony in his soliloquy. Instead, he reveals that he is determined to deal severely with his spouse: 'This humor must I holde me to a while,/ To bridle and hold backe my headstrong wife.' She, too, will be denied food and sleep; but, in addition, she will remain imprisoned until she has been thoroughly broken:

> I'll mew her up as men do mew their hawkes,
> And make her gentlie come unto the lure,
> Were she as stuborne or as full of strength

---

16 John C. Bean, 'Comic Structure and the Humanizing of Kate in The Taming of The Shrew,' The Woman's Part, edited by Carolyn Lenz, Gayle Greene, and Carol Neely, pp. 65–78.

As were the *Thracian* horse *Alcides* tamde,
That King *Egeus* fed with flesh of men,
Yet would I pull her downe and make her come
As hungry hawkes do flie unto there lure.   (ix.46–52)

The emphasis in his speech is on his determination, no matter how long it takes, to force her to accept permanent submission. He has not even a passing thought for her happiness or for the effect his plan of action must have on their future relationship. And rather than suggesting that the change in her manner and outlook will make her a happier person, this husband stresses his ability to hold out until he gets everything he wants. His male chauvinism is unrelieved by humor or self-awareness, and his use of the bird-taming imagery refers only to its harshest elements of domination, persistence, and insistence.

For our purposes, understanding how the behavior of the hero reflects his feelings is more valuable than appreciating the playwright's knowledge of how to tame wild creatures. But as it turns out, according to the foremost authority on the subject, the proper feelings and motivation are essential if a bird-tamer is to be successful. George Turberville in *The Booke of Faulconrie or Hawking* (1575), the most influential and popular study of this subject, stresses the importance of the rapport between falconer and falcon, emphasizing the need for attention and care as well as insisting that the character and temperament of the trainer are directly related to the results he achieves:

> And here I thinke good to expresse mine opinion, that hee whiche taketh in hande to bee a Falconer, ought firste to bee verye patient, and therewithall to take singular delight in an Hawke, so that hee may seeme to bee in love (as it were naturally) with his Hawke, even that a man would say, it were a thing bredde so in the bone as it coulde never bee rooted oute of the fleshe. For such a man with never so little paine and industrie, will become an excellent Falconer: but hee whiche taketh not that delight in his Hawke, but doeth rather exercise it for a pompe and boast, than uppon a naturall instinct ... such a man in mine opinion shall seldome prove a perfeite Falconer.[17]

Petruchio, one must assume, is not motivated by the desire for 'a pompe and boast,' but rather by 'a singular delight' that at the very least approximates the love between the trainer and his bird described by Turberville.[18]

The mutual dependency of hawk and tamer as well as their interreliance, their shared trust, and their sympathetic concern are qualities that describe the best marriages. In addition, the relationship of bird and tamer perfectly parallels the Elizabethan injunctions in the 'Homily on Marriage' concerning the obedience, gentleness, and submission that

---

[17] P. 142.
[18] See Margaret Loftus Ranald, 'The Manning of the Haggard; or, *The Taming of The Shrew,' Essays in Literature* (Fall, 1974) 1:149–165. According to Ranald, the real value of the hawking imagery 'lies in its emphasizing the fact that the taming of a wild, mature falcon aims at achieving mutual respect between bird and keeper' (p. 153).

wives traditionally owed to their husbands. The following episodes in which Katherine is denied her dinner, her cap, and her gown are dramatizations of Petruchio's putting theory into practice. Katherine finally relinquishes her opposition to his will when, with a kind of bemused weariness – and possibly with not a little admiration for his persistence – she accepts Hortensio's advice to second whatever Petruchio says. As much a mocker as her husband, Katherine quickly discovers that absolute agreement with her husband's judgment, especially when his view contradicts her own, means she can enjoy a delightful irresponsibility.

This new and highly pleasing discovery is demonstrated in the very next scene. In obedience to Petruchio, who calls the old traveller Vincentio a 'fair lovely maid,' Katherine addresses the elderly gentleman first as a 'young budding virgin, fair, and fresh, and sweet.' Then, following her husband's new lead, she recognizes Vincentio as 'a reverend father.' Although surprised by their extraordinary behavior, Vincentio realizes that this young couple is simply high-spirited, whimsically humorous, and in absolute agreement: Petruchio is a 'fair sir' and Katherine is his 'merry mistress.' This shared delight in quick-witted inventiveness, demonstrating how rather complex characters come to affectionate understanding of one another, is characteristic of Shakespearean lovers and signifies just how well-suited they are. Katherine can match Petruchio's capriciousness with a clever rejoinder:

> Pardon, old father, my mistaking eyes,
> That have been so bedazzled with the sun
> That everything I look on seemeth green.   (IV.v.44–46)

In the Shakespearean treatment we are shown the new harmony of the lovers, affirming the understanding that is its basis in the last private conversation of the pair. Still sensitive to public opinion, Katherine is reluctant to kiss her husband in the street:

> Kath: Husband, let's follow to see the end of this ado.
> Pet: First kiss me, Kate, and we will.
> Kath: What, in the midst of the street?
> Pet: What, art thou ashamed of me?
> Kath: No, sir, God forbid; but ashamed to kiss.   (V.i.130–134)

How very different from her behavior when Petruchio first asked for a kiss! Now in her judgment he is no longer a 'mad-brain rudesby,' nor does she believe because of her husband she has made the 'world point at poor Katherine.' Katherine not only kisses him but enjoys it, admitting she takes pleasure in his company. As Brian Morris points out in the Arden edition, for the first time their affection for one another appears genuine in both word and deed.[19]

---

[19] P. 286.

The final demonstration of the basis for their happy marriage occurs in the problematic last scene of the play. This begins with the three newly married pairs assembled in celebration at a banquet. In exchanging pleasantries and jokes, Hortensio's new bride turns one of Petruchio's innocent remarks into a rather more critical observation. She says that her marriage to Hortensio is quite different from what Petruchio thinks; according to her, Petruchio is hardly one to comment on her marriage since 'He that is giddy thinks the world turns round.' Her words trouble Katherine, who demands an explanation and receives one that does not please her:

> Kath: 'He that is giddy thinks the world turns round' –
>   I pray you tell me what you meant by that.
> Wid: Your husband, being troubled with a shrew,
>   Measures my husband's sorrow by his woe.
>   And now you know my meaning.
> Kath: A very mean meaning.
> Wid: Right, I mean you.
> Kath: And I am mean, indeed, respecting you.   (V.ii.26–32)

After the women leave the stage, the husbands begin to plan the terms of the wager that will prove whose wife is most obedient. With this brief prologue to the obedience-test, we should hardly be surprised that Katherine acts with unsurpassed humility. We have repeatedly seen that she is concerned with what others will think of her, and she could hardly be pleased either for herself or her husband that the world imagines hers to be an unhappy marriage. The wager is the perfect opportunity for her to prove the world wrong, and she demonstrates her deference to Petruchio's will by her immediate response to his summons. Moreover, unlike the other new husbands, Petruchio does not 'bid' or 'entreat' his wife to attend him; rather, he orders Grumio to 'command her to come to me.' Katherine could hardly fail to hear the difference among these three verbs, and, unlike the less well-trained new brides, she responds immediately to his order. She is proving that she is what she calls in her summing-up speech 'obedient to his honest will.' Petruchio is not demanding that she commit any deed that would be what Cordelia describes as a 'vicious blot' on her nature; 'murther or foulness,/ No unchaste action, or dishonour'd step.' If in Petruchio's judgment her cap is unbecoming, if, having paid for it, he would rather have it thrown under foot, then obeying his request is merely proof that Katherine prefers to be yielding and attractive in his eyes.

Her second action, offering her hand to help her husband and placing it below his foot, points up another quality of their marriage. Their relationship depends not simply on mutual deference but also on trust: she would risk hurting herself to help him; yet he would not hurt her, and she knows he would not hurt her. Indeed, he has never once punished her physically – even after she struck him. This differs significantly from the similar action in *A Shrew* which demonstrated the total self-abasement of the wife in marriage. In the Shakespearean version, a successful marriage requires both deference and trust: Katherine's behavior shows that she now understands this and her speech explains why she believes hers to be the correct conduct.

Her words are a lesson in proper wifely behavior to those just married. Following Elizabethan precedent of reasoning by analogy, she proves that a wife is to her husband as a subject is to the prince. She who refuses to give 'love, fair looks, and true obedience' to her husband is 'a foul contending rebel,/ A graceless traitor,' offering 'war' when she 'should kneel for peace.' Katherine closes this line of her argument by restating the words of the marriage ceremony according to the Book of Common Prayer: wives 'are bound to serve, love, and obey.'

Kate's next line of argument is that a woman's physical weakness, 'unapt to toil and trouble in the world,' requires her to give place to her husband, whose superior strength enables him to subject 'his body/ To painful labour' for her ease and comfort. Although she acknowledges women's physical inferiority, we should notice particularly that Katherine grants men no moral or intellectual superiority. She speaks of a woman's role in terms of duty, amiability, obedience, gentleness, and trust, yet she never claims men excel women in anything more than brawn and muscle. Katherine never suggests that women are in any way morally or intellectually inferior to men. In her speech, Shakespeare's heroine stresses the grace and beauty that a wife contributes to marriage with 'love and fair looks.' As her husband is responsible for her welfare, so she returns his care by being 'obedient to his honest will,' and by managing a home in which they can enjoy happiness, not 'bandy word for word and frown for frown.' The play insists on the need for mutual responsibility, on the need to join femininity – 'bodies soft, and weak, and smooth' – with masculinity – for a man must be strong who 'commits his body / To painful labour both by sea and land.' Each sex needs the other for true fulfillment. The misogyny that characterizes the view in *A Shrew* finds no support in *The Shrew*. Rather, Shakespeare's play points out the husband's obligations to the wife as well as the reverse, and it develops the Renaissance theory of the love of prince and subject as a parallel to the relationship of husband and wife; as the action develops the play seems in agreement with the more liberal writers on the role of women in marriage.

At the same time, none of this seems ultraliberal in its position on women's rights – Katherine, too, we will recall, places her hand beneath her husband's foot to demonstrate her readiness to 'do him ease.' Yet, the comparable speech in *A Shrew* presents a view of women that is still far less complimentary and more critical, for there the speaker based her assessment of the character of women on an anti-feminist interpretation of *Genesis*. Women as the source of sin and death, the curse of mankind, are surely very different beings from those described by Shakespeare's heroine. Katherine is no longer a shrew, a role that clearly did not make her happy; she is now a contented wife. Yet even in her corrected understanding of the proper relationship of husbands and wives, even in her

well-adjusted appreciation of the appropriate behavior and responsibilities of both marriage partners, Katherine maintains in comparison with
her contemporaries of both sexes, a very high notion of the abilities of
women.

Katherine's closing speech can properly be interpreted neither as a
conditioned reflex, as some critics have proposed, nor as an example of
her public humiliation.[20] Rather, it expresses her understanding that her
happiness is a consequence of accepting the traditional role of a wife. In
this regard, the view presented in The Taming of the Shrew is far more moderate than that found in A Shrew, dramatizing a conception of marriage
close to the more liberal Protestantism of Henry Smith. For example,
Smith argues that 'husbands must hold their hands and wives their tungs,'
and, rather like Petruchio, he thinks

> the best policy in marriage is to begin well, ... to learne one anothers nature,
> and one anothers affections, and one anothers infirmities, because ye must
> be helpers, and ye cannot help, unlesse ye know the disease. Al the jarres
> almost which do trouble this band [of marriage], do rise of this, that one
> dooth not hit the measure of the others heart, to applie themselves to either
> nature. ... Therefore they must learne ... to fashion themselves one to the
> other.[21]

This 'fashioning' process is dramatized on the road to Padua when
Katherine and Petruchio meet Vincentio and discover how to 'hit the
measure of the others heart.' Indeed, the concern for mutual happiness is
common to both Smith and The Shrew. Petruchio tells us of his behavior to
Katherine: 'I intend/ That all is done in reverend care of her' (IV.i.
191–192); and Katherine instructs the other brides that wives 'are bound
to serve, love, and obey' their husbands (V.ii.165). Partners in the most
successful marriages strive not to dominate but rather to make one
another happy.

In this partnership, Katherine can enjoy her husband's high spirits, his
lively, impulsive, and playful nature by matching wits with him in inventiveness and imagination. To Petruchio's absurd vision of Vincentio as a
sweet, young maid, she can add an elaborate comparative: 'Happy the
parents of so fair a child,/ Happier the man whom favourable stars/ Allots
thee for his lovely bedfellow.' The joy in this game is in returning the
serve; and our pleasure in watching, as theirs in playing, comes from
the perfect matching of the abilities of the participants, their sense of
humor and intelligence. But in larger terms, the game they are enjoying is
marriage and our delight is in the demonstration of a marriage of true
minds.

---

[20] In his article John Bean sums up much of the critical commentary on this important
speech. For a recent and highly personal interpretation, see Linda Woodbridge, Women and
the English Renaissance, pp. 206–207.
[21] Pp. 58–59.

The Woman's Prize or, The Tamer Tam'd (1611) by John Fletcher directly treats the theme of the shrew-in-marriage by dramatizing the post-nuptial trials of the widower Petruchio after his second wedding. Fletcher is cleverly reworking a popular subject, for Shakespeare's play remained in the repertory of the King's Men after 1610, and, according to the Master of the Revels, Sir Henry Herbert, it was even 'liked' by Charles I and Henrietta Maria when acted at Court on 26 November 1633.[22] Fletcher's play proved even more popular, for Herbert reported that it was 'very well liked' by the Court when it was performed two days after Shakespeare's comedy.

Fletcher's subtitle indicates that he is consciously turning the tables on Shakespeare's hero; and, indeed, Petruchio's new bride, Maria, is determined to reverse roles with Shakespeare's Kate. Maria will spare no effort to subdue her new husband, who she knows is 'famous for a woman tamer/ And ... a brave wife-breaker,' and she will continue to thwart him until she renders him as 'easie as a child.' As she explains, her goal is to train her husband to such a yielding nature that 'spight of all the freedom he has reach'd to, [I will] turn him and bend him as I list, and mold him/ Into a babe again; that aged women,/ Wanting teeth and spleen, may Master him.'

At the opening of the play, Maria claims that the mere 'disobedience of a wife' is insufficient to describe her aim:

> You talk too tamely: By the faith I have
> In mine own Noble will, that childish woman
> That lives a prisoner to her husbands pleasure,
> Has lost her making, and becomes a beast,
> Created for his use, not fellowship.   (I.ii.135–139)

And she demonstrates the extent of her defiance and stamina first by physically fortifying herself against her husband and his besieging friends. Yet, even after he has agreed to all her demands for liberty, clothes, coaches, and jewels, she refuses to consummate the marriage. Next, when Petruchio feigns illness, she out-feigns him by pretending that he has the plague and has him sealed in his house as contagious. Afterwards, admitting that she has 'been a little peevish .../ Only to try your temper,' she nevertheless continues to be contrary: when Petruchio threatens to leave her and travel abroad, she urges him to go rather than stay with her. When, as a last ploy, Petruchio presents himself as dead in his coffin, killed by unrequited love, Maria still berates his 'corpse' for his faults. At this point, exhausted and outwitted, offering no defense for himself except love for her, Petruchio claims he will 'die indeed' unless she will truly live with him as his wife. Now Maria makes a complete reversal of the convictions she has defended for the previous four acts:

---

[22] H. J. Oliver, introduction to The Taming of The Shrew, p. 64.

> I have done my worst, and have my end, forgive me;
> From this houre make me what you please: I have tam'd ye,
> And now am vowd your servant.
> ...
>   As I am honest,
> And as I am a maid yet, all my life
> From this houre, since ye make so free profession,
> I dedicate in service to your pleasure.   (V.iv.44–57)

This is the 'husband's pleasure' she had so adamantly refused at the opening of the play. The grounds of her refusal, however, are difficult to understand, if not entirely incomprehensible. Maria concedes to her husband more than Petruchio has ever asked of her:

> I urge not service from you, nor obedience
> In way of duty, but of love, and credit
> All I expect is but a noble care
> Of what I have brought you, and of what I am,
> And what our name may be.   (III.iii.104–108)

Despite his reputation as a martinet, Petruchio is a man of modest expectations, and he never demonstrates sufficient justification for Maria's contrariness.

This confusion between action and intention, a kind of misalignment between cause and effect, is a major flaw in the dramaturgy here. Often we are quite unsure why characters do what they do, just as we may not fully understand why at certain times they stop and suddenly find themselves in agreement. The reason for the conflict between Maria and Petruchio is never truly explained or dramatized, and, for all we can tell, it has no real basis. The sequence of incidents that should prove, test, and finally resolve their opposition – the fortified resistance, the feigned illness, the fake death – do not develop theme or character. We have no sense here that the husband or wife understands the appropriateness of behavior of Shakespeare's Petruchio, who will kill a humor by imitating it. Maria's actions merely demonstrate the same point. We discover no growing awareness, no heightened consciousness, no emerging sensitivity on the part of either of the characters. In addition, the episodes are not integrated; one completed action follows another until sufficient amusement has been provided for the play to reach its conclusion.[23] One finds no inherent logic in the sequence of events. Maria might as well fortify herself in a barricaded house as a last, climactic, all-out effort against Petruchio than do this as the first proof of her resistance. According to the Prologue, 'The end we ayme at, is to make you sport,' and this is, perhaps, the best explanation for the choice and ordering of the incidents.

But even in the nature of its laughter, Fletcher's comedy presents difficulties. The source of its humor is not frivolous enough to be innocent

---

[23] See Cyrus Hoy, 'Fletcherian Romantic Comedy,' *Research Opportunities in Renaissance Drama* (1984), 27:3–11.

and hearty, nor well-observed enough to mock the serious incongruities and obstacles to happiness in marriage. The play's tone is too harsh, too jarring if its aim is merely to make 'sport.' When Petruchio warns Maria that her unreasonable, obstinate, and willful behavior well merits some forceful response from him, she threatens to retaliate in so fierce a manner that all comic possibilities are destroyed:

> I defie you.
> And my last loving teares farwell: the first stroke,
> The very first you give me, if you dare strike,
> Try me, and you shall finde it so, for ever
> Never to be recall'd: I know you love me,
> Mad till you have enjoy'd me; I doe turne
> Utterly from you, and what man I meet first
> That has but spirit to deserve a favour,
> Let him beare any shape, the worse the better,
> Shall kill you, and enjoy me.　　　　　　　　　　(IV.ii.142–151)

In addition, as this speech suggests, much of the laughter is based on Maria's successful denying of her favors and on Petruchio's frustration and embarrassment:

> Sophocles: Not let you touch her all this night?
> Petruchio:　　　 Not touch her.
> Sophocles: Where was your courage?
> Petruchio:　　　 Where was her obedience?
> 　　　　　Never poore man was sham'd so; never Rascall
> 　　　　　That keeps a stud of whores was us'd so basely.　　(III.iii.1–4)

This method of Maria's for taming Petruchio is discussed well beyond the level of light-hearted comedy. In fact, the attention given to this aspect of the struggle for dominance between husband and wife is so great that the dialogue approaches the indecent:

> Sophocles:　　 It may be then,
> 　　　　Her modesty requir'd a little violence?
> 　　　　Some women love to struggle.
> Petruchio:　　 She had it,
> 　　　　And so much that I sweat for't, so I did,
> 　　　　But to no end: I washt an Ethiope,
> 　　　　She swore no force might weary her, but win her
> 　　　　I never could, nor should, till she consented.
> 　　　　　　...
> Sophocles:　　 Tis strange;
> 　　　　This woman is the first I ever read of,
> 　　　　Refus'd a warranted occasion,
> 　　　　And standing on so fair terms.　　　　　　(III.iii.8–18)

Continuing his account of his predicament, Petruchio offers details that reveal both the crudeness of his behavior and the coarseness of his wife's responses:

```
Petruchio:        I swore unto her,
                  And by no little ones, if presently
                  Without more disputation on the matter,
                  She grew not neerer to me, and dispatcht me
                  Out of the pain I was, (for I was nettl'd)
                  And willingly, and eagerly, and sweetly,
                  I would go to her Chamber-maid, and in her hearing
                  Begin her such a huntes-up.
Sophocles:        Then she started?
Petruchio:  No more then I do now; marry she answered
                  If I were so dispos'd, she could not help it
                  But there was one cal'd Jaques, a poor Butler,
                  One that might content a single woman
Sophocles:  And he should tilt her?
Petruchio:        To that sence, and last
                  She bade me yet these six nights look for nothing,
                  Nor strive to purchase it.              (III.iii.19–33)
```

Perhaps no single factor better points up the difference between Shakespeare's treatment of the story and Fletcher's than the absence in Shakespeare of any discussion of the consummation of the marriage.

The defects we have noted in character, plotting, and tone in The Woman's Prize are finally rounded out by the play's failure to reconcile these elements with its announced intention. According to the Epilogue, the work means to demonstrate that husbands 'should not raigne as Tyrants o'r their wives' just as wives must not 'Insult, or triumph' over their husbands. The lesson of the play is 'aptly meant,/ To teach both Sexes due equality;/ And as they stand bound, to love mutually.' But Fletcher's Epilogue is not supported by his dramaturgy. The announced theme relates the play closely to the approach we have found in Shakespeare's endorsement of marriage as a mutual concern. But as we saw earlier, a major obstacle to finding this theme central to the play itself is that Maria completely rejects it when Petruchio proposes it to her in III.iii., and the final reconciliation should require neither an apology nor a promise of dedicated 'service to your pleasure' such as Maria offers to Petruchio in Act V. Whatever he may have thought the play was saying, Fletcher in his Epilogue does not sum up the meaning of the work. On the contrary, Fletcher's shrew-taming wife Maria is, in fact, a shrew in her own right, and his Petruchio is a frustrated railer who boasts of his reputation and strength even while he complains of his sexual frustration and weakness. Neither character develops as a consequence of experience; transformation replaces growth. Sustaining the dramatic interest through confrontation and opposition is the determining principle of the plotting, and spicing this with references to sexual conduct or to Maria's refusal to consummate her marriage adds further piquancy to the action. Finally, passing all this off with a few concluding words about 'equality' between the sexes and about mutual love as the basis of a happy marriage is merely an attempt to add an intellectual gloss to threadbare material that has not a shred of an idea. Fletcher, for his easy facility with words, is neither the playwright as thinker nor the playwright as psychologist. Rather, this most productive and popular of Jacobean dramatists is the playwright as opportunist and technician.

As we have seen, the proper relations between husbands and wives and the proper conduct of women in marriage are subjects that may be dramatized through the presentation of the type character of the shrew. For this reason, we may suspect that the contradictory attitudes found in Fletcher's play and its ambiguous conclusion may reflect some of the irreconcilable elements that were prevalent in Protestant thought in the early seventeenth century. The difficulty in *The Woman's Prize* is that while it advocates mutual concern as the basis of happiness in marriage it also promotes the notion that wives should be totally subservient to their husbands. Perhaps the play is responding to inconsistencies in Protestantism itself. On the one hand, Protestant theologians justified the notion of patriarchy which, in turn, gave greater emphasis to the husband's role as head of the household: 'the consequence was ... the legal rights of women actually diminished.' At the same time, Protestantism also endorsed the notion of mutual affection in marriage which gave greater emphasis to women's rights. 'By stressing mutual affection and male domination in marriage Protestantism set up a tension. It proved fatal in [Milton's] paradise and must have been difficult for many in the seventeenth century.[24] *The Women's Prize* manages to endorse both contradictory claims. We should appreciate the play's awareness and sensitivity to these two opposing strains of Protestant thought even as we recognize the impossibility of reconciling them. Nevertheless, the drama's ability to give expression to an especially full range of opinion is undoubtedly one of the reasons for its success.

Although we cannot expect a play to provide a solution for the strains of marriage, we might demand more coherence and integration in a work of art than its author has taken the trouble to supply in *The Woman's Prize*. Its weaknesses, however, do not detract from the significance of its contribution to the evolution of a type of witty romantic comedy, for Fletcher is furthering the development of a highly sophisticated treatment of the question of which partner will retain dominance in marriage and at what price. Without Fletcher's plays we cannot be sure that this subject matter would have received its most polished form in the comedies that were acted just before the close of the seventeenth century, when Congreve refined and molded the theme and characters Fletcher had, in effect, prepared for him. The jousting of Petruchio and Maria is transmuted into the witty combats of Mirabell and Millamant, the demands of Maria are metamorphosed into the provisos of the Restoration lovers, and her final yielding 'in service to your pleasure' is rephrased as the concession that a woman may 'by degrees dwindle into a wife.'

---

[24] Alan Sinfield, *Literature in Protestant England 1560–1660*, pp. 65–70

VII

Conclusion

Each of the character types we have discussed has provided insight into a different aspect of Renaissance society: the courtier demonstrates appropriate courtly behavior; the savage man points up the variety of responses to civilization and its discontents; the overreacher raises questions about ambition and the values of the good life; the Machiavel and the Tool Villain offer comment on issues of political morality and expediency; and the shrew focuses attention on the proper role of women in marriage and on the proper relations between the sexes. By considering the differing presentations of these type characters in Renaissance drama in relation to some of the most influential philosophical and intellectual writings of the time, we have seen how social attitudes may affect dramatic characterization.

In dramatizing the ideal courtier for a courtly audience, John Lyly in *Campaspe* naturally presented his hero, Alexander the Great, as one who embodied the conservative, aristocratic, and idealized code of behavior of Elizabeth herself. Alexander may reveal his humanity by his feelings for Campaspe, but he proves his nobility by showing self-restraint and self-control. He can only be Alexander by suppressing his emotions, rejecting Campaspe, and returning to the battlefield. As Sir Thomas Elyot stresses in *The Governour*, duty must always come first. In the play, too, the hero can only be heroic by demonstrating how highly he regards those obligations and responsibilities that come with positions of leadership.

As further proof of Alexander's will power and, no doubt, as a compliment to a ruler who had strong passions and attachments herself, Lyly's hero points out that those of royal blood can repress or frustrate their own personal desires only by exercising a more than common degree of self-discipline: Alexander expects our sympathy and respect because 'in a great prince ... passions and thoughts do as far exceede others in extremitie, as their callings doe in majestie.' This self-discipline is especially difficult to achieve, but, after all, Alexander could hardly expect 'to commaund the world if he could not commaund himself.'

Like Lyly's hero, Shakespeare's Hal is also tempted to leave the path of courtly virtue. But unlike *Campaspe*, which presents a single, straightforward version of the courtier, *Henry IV, Part One* dramatizes the conflict that arises when differing notions of proper courtly behavior are set against one another. The narrowness of Hotspur's conception of what befits a courtier – honor, chiefly won through battle – is contrasted with both Hal's and Falstaff's views on conduct. Hotspur has clearly not cut his cloth after the latest Renaissance design, for his obsession with honor is far more limited than that of any role model described by either Elyot or Castiglione, the two most influential writers on this subject.

Hal, as 'king of courtesy,' follows the pattern largely established as an ideal in *The Courtier* where courtesy, winning ways, gallantry, gaiety, and grace are highly prized. In addition, Castiglione praises a lively mind and a rambunctious sense of humor, two more qualities Hal fully demonstrates. Although he embodies the principal character traits required to fulfill Elyot's notion of the perfect courtier, Hal's ease and charm are, perhaps, more than can be subsumed by Elyot's terms of 'affability' and 'placibility.' And even his deviousness is a trait not inappropriate for one who plans a political career. All in all, the madcap Prince of Wales actually seems a hero designed more after the latest Italian models than according to the more sober English fashion.

Falstaff, however, is always his own man. He will live by no one else's values: honor and courtesy are fine terms only if they allow one to enjoy life. High ideals and political ambitions are all well and good, but a case must be made for the pleasures of the senses and for the delights of the flesh. And surely no one is better able to make that case than the fat knight. Self-preservation and self-indulgence are the goals of his philosophy of conduct.

This chronicle history dramatizes considerably more than simply the early years of the madcap Prince of Wales. In the course of the play, the hero manages to acquire all the most admired and desirable attributes of the perfect courtier, and his achievement is made particularly distinctive by its juxtaposition with the actions of Hotspur and Falstaff. Moreover, events prove the truth that a leader can best succeed by making others want to follow him, and the future Henry V demonstrates that he has just this ability.

Dekker follows the route of Shakespeare's success by providing a fresh embodiment of Falstaff in the shoemaker, Simon Eyre, and by bringing the popular Henry V back onto the stage. His hero, Rowland Lacy, also fails to live up to the ideals of courtly behavior and promises reformation. But although *The Shoemaker's Holiday* was acted at court soon after Shakespeare's play, Dekker's king and courtier seem to know nothing of the recommendations of Elyot or Castiglione and to care even less for the strict views on commitment and responsibility of Lyly's Alexander. For example, the heroine of Lyly's comedy understood that she would not be happy marrying outside of her class, but the happiness of the lovers in Dekker's play results from the denial of class distinctions. Yet, despite the denial of such distinctions, we are shown how class has its privilege: Ralph, the newlywed shoemaker, must go off to war to fulfill his military obligations; but by sending a substitute, Rowland Lacy can stay home and woo his sweetheart. Ralph returns crippled to find his wife has disappeared, but Lacy, pretending to be a shoemaker, ultimately manages to marry Rose and be knighted by the king he failed to serve. In this inconsistent and sentimental view of things, one cannot find any notion of proper conduct or responsible behavior.

Affairs of the heart are quite naturally treated with importance in a romantic comedy, and we expect them to have a happy resolution. But the questionable morality of the romantic intrigue here is matched by the equally dubious morality practiced in the marketplace. In effect, Simon Eyre's impersonation of an alderman, the fraud that really starts him on the road to commercial success, is as immoral as Rowland Lacy's disguise as a shoemaker. Evidently, we are meant to judge both gentlemen alike, for both are handsomely rewarded through their deceptions. Matters of right and wrong in conduct as in all of life seem easily determined by a pragmatic approach: what is right is simply what one can get away with. And lest that view of life appear too harsh, it is glossed over by the bonhomie of Eyre and the songs of his workers. As Alexander Leggatt has remarked, 'The impression that lingers in the memory, after a casual perusal of the play, is that Simon Eyre became Lord Mayor of London because he was a jolly and energetic shoemaker.'[1] The bustle and high spirits of the action enable Dekker 'to show Eyre as an example to proper social behaviour, ... innocent of greed or guile.'[2] But, in fact, the self-interest and social irresponsibility rewarded in The Shoemaker's Holiday demonstrate how greatly notions of proper conduct were changing and how profoundly traditional values were being displaced. This comedy anticipates the Jacobean age well before James VI set out for London, and it reminds us that the new king did not impose his values on the English but rather found a population already receptive to the standards of conduct that would be practiced in his court.

Unlike the character type of the courtier, the genus of the savage man may belong to one of three species. Moreover, within each species the range of representation and interpretation is broad indeed. The first category of these, the Bremo or Caliban figure, for example, may serve either simply as a clown, providing low comedy, or as a means of questioning the nature of civilization. To consider the more complex instance, Caliban focuses our attention on the differences between savagery and cultured humanity, which involve knowing how to find satisfaction and freedom through submission and restraint. And at the same time, he also blurs the simple,

---

[1] Citizen Comedy in the Age of Shakespeare, p. 19.
[2] P. 13.

clear-cut contrast between the civilized and the wild: *The Tempest* contains a pair of European nobles who are villains far more conscious of their wickedness and so far more evil than this creature for whom right and wrong seem to be relatively new concepts.

In the second category of savage man, we find the human child reared in a state of nature. The early play, based on the *Valentine and Orson* story, emphasizes adventure and breeding; Orson, though nurtured by a bear and brought up in the forest, is innately noble because he is of noble birth. And the happy conclusion, accomplished through the instructions of a brazen head, provides little to help us understand why these things should be. *Cymbeline*, however, treats matters of heredity and environment with much greater care and attention. Cymbeline's sons brought up in the rough hills of Wales are as gentle and courtly as the noble orphan Posthumus brought up at court. In sharp contrast, the king's step-son, Cloten, is both foolish and wicked. Clearly, matters of environment and heredity are not so simply explained after all. And in the resolution to the action, the play attempts to address philosophical questions about the rationale of the gods in bestowing their gifts, for fortune and nature seem never to agree. In *Cymbeline*, Jupiter explains that we taste the sweetness of joy with even greater pleasure when we have first known the bitterness of sorrow: Posthumus shall be 'happier much by this affliction made.' His words remind one of those speeches in *Pericles*, where the hero, finally reunited with his daughter, thinks of his 'past miseries' as 'sport.' Once again, former sorrows only intensify present happiness.

The last distinct species of the savage man we considered is the civilized individual who has reverted to a state of nature because of his mental anguish. Naturally, the playwright's subtlety in presenting a finely shaded portrait of growing alienation and disillusionment, in dramatizing the hero's deepening revulsion against humanity that ripens into despair and even madness, determines the quality and power of the presentation.

This type of savage man's rejection of civilization and human society is never condoned in *King Lear* or *Pericles*, for the heroes in those works must fully accept their humanity along with the pain and joy that only human beings are capable of experiencing. Indeed, by knowing sorrow and happiness they come to be fully human, by offering love and compassion they demonstrate their humanity, and by granting forgiveness and reconciliation they practice the highest virtues.

Through Edgar, who is reduced to Poor Tom and who ends the play as king, we are witnesses to the great range of man's potential roles in life just as through Lear's family we discover the enormous possibilites of human behavior, from the savage to the angelic. And by dramatizing man's capacity to feel and suffer as well as to forget and forgive, *King Lear* examines the crucial question of how man is ultimately distinguished from the animal world to which he partially belongs. Robert Greene's *Orlando Furioso*, with its comically deranged hero, is a poor foil for Shakespeare's artistry in *Pericles* and *Lear*.

Like the character type of the savage man, the overreacher can offer serious statements about the human condition. Since the range of religious and philosophic views about man's potential was so vast, from Pico's notion that we are 'constrained by no limits' to Calvin's insistence that 'we are not our own,' Renaissance drama could use the overreacher as a means of portraying the proper goals of humanity. How one achieves the good life and what ambitions are most satisfying are two of the questions that the career of the overreacher seems to be addressing.

Tamburlaine, for example, presents an overreacher for whom the 'sweet fruition of an earthly crown' is about the only worthwhile endeavor. The struggle and excitement, the richness and exoticism of unending conquests over foreign lands are the only activities that can satisfy the restless nature of this overreacher. Even though he must yield ultimately to death, the Tamburlaine-figure must constantly test himself, proving his energy and his ability.

An ultimate lack of self-fulfillment also awaits the more sophisticated overreacher, Faustus. He comes to realize that neither of the two options open to him will provide him with a life that is satisfying. On the one hand, his total self-indulgence – 24 years of serving his own appetite – leaves him worthless and degraded, reduced to a mere trickster and a clown. On the other hand, were he to obey the prohibitions and requirements of the severe and unforgiving divinity in the heavens, who demands self-denial and self-abasement, Faustus would also be left feeling degraded. In Marlowe's view of matters, frustration and anguish are the emotions that inevitably attend the human condition.

In these plays man's discontent can be blamed on the nature of things; for him, something is inherently out of order on a metaphysical level. In contrast, in The Alchemist the problem is not metaphysical: the difficulty lies in the character of man himself, a being self-seeking and corrupt. Fallen man, however, can take correction from the truthfulness of nature. Since the metaphysical structure of the universe is sound, nature works to disclose the truth. Although man may prefer to ignore or deny the fundamental truthfulness of nature, he cannot ultimately succeed in perverting her honesty.

Having this unshakable belief in the perfectibility of nature, Jonson's satire demonstrates how futile and foolish are man's attempts to corrupt her. Motivated by greed, a drive he can scarcely keep under control, Jonsonian mankind tries to hoodwink the world into serving his own desires: indeed, most deceivers thrive for a time simply by pretending to serve the avariciousness of their gulls. But ultimately both dupes and dupers are uncovered.

Jonson's overreacher, Sir Epicure Mammon, is the consummate solipsist. In his mind, the world exists only to gratify his insatiable appetite for wealth, sex, and self-indulgence; at the same time, Subtle, Face, and Dol think that they can satisfy their interests by pretending to pander to his. In the end, all are disappointed, for they have attempted to pervert nature to their own purposes. Like Marlowe's overreachers, they are frustrated by life. But unlike their predecessors, they are subjects of laughter and contempt, for they are fools who do not realize that the universe is truthful, just, and consistent. Jonson's belief in a metaphysical ideal enables him to present the character type of the overreacher as a figure of satiric amusement rather than as a tragic hero.

Shakespeare's version of the overreacher in *The Tempest* is unique among our examples, for Prospero alone seems to have found a means to achieve true contentment at the end of the play. He would not dwell on the unhappy past – 'Let us not burthen our remembrance' with/ A heaviness that's gone' – and he can even bring himself to forgive those whose wickedness has been extreme. He can practice the compassion that Ariel feels for those shipwrecked on the island, and he can exercise the 'nobler reason' that turns away from revenge. Once again, to forget and forgive seem crucial ingredients for happiness.

Essential for his true happiness, however, is Prospero's rejection of the power that made him an overreacher, a power that could bedim the sun, call forth the wind and sea, and even wake the dead. Prospero must decide to 'abjure' his 'great magic,' and become as other men. Instead of withdrawing from society, he determines to return to Milan to take up his rightful position. He comes to realize that by fulfilling his duties and by accepting the limitations of mankind he can find true contentment. By his conduct, Prospero suggests that the greatest satisfaction we can achieve is ultimately derived from the complete acceptance of our humanity, with all of its failings. The boldness and daring of the overreacher may seem exciting and admirable, but his isolation from his fellows and his desire for the infinite can never lead to real happiness – that results only from the wisdom to live fully as a human being.

The last representative of this character type, Massinger's Sir Giles Overreach, is both the least daring and the least intellectual example. Sir Giles wants to conquer no new worlds, to experience no new sensual pleasures, or even to scale no new intellectual heights. Indeed, his ambition hardly seems to qualify him as an overreacher – his family name notwithstanding – for, in fact, he is obsessed with the simple notion of making his only daughter a great lady, a 'Right honorable.' Actually, his claim to membership in this category of type characters rests not so much on his intention as on the intensity of his obsession. Sir Giles fully expects to marry his child to Lord Lovell; but frustrated, he gives way to a terrifying madness that is both ferocious and moralistic. He rants like a helpless Tamburlaine:

> though Hercules call it odds,
> I'll stand against both, as I am hemmed in thus.
> Since, like Libyan lion in the toil,
> My fury cannot reach the coward hunters,
> And only spends itself, I'll quit the place. (V.i.307–311)

The reason for his insanity is interpreted for us by Lord Lovell as a lesson to the wicked that their crimes will not pay: when 'wicked men ... leave religion, and turn atheists,/ Their own abilities leave 'em.'

In fact, Massinger's drama offers this moral gratuitously, for the play has nowhere demonstrated it. Massinger's Sir Giles is simply a monstrously determined capitalist with social pretensions. There is nothing complex about him. He has none of the ambiguously admirable qualities of the Marlovian hero, none of the ludicrously satiric traits of the Jonsonian butt, and none of the deeply compassionate understanding of the Shakespearean white magician. Unlike them, Massinger's overreacher does not reject society's values for his own; on the contrary, he is determined to judge his accomplishments by the most conservative and traditionally accepted social criteria – moving up the social scale by marrying his daughter into the aristocracy. The overreacher has been reduced to a compulsive social climber.

As we have seen, the presentation of the overreacher may be colored by the work of a variety of religious and philosophical writers who held widely differing views of the nature of man and who proposed mutually incompatible definitions of the good life. But all of the examples of the character types of the Machiavel and the Tool Villain have a common origin in the writings of Machiavelli or in the commentaries on The Prince, and all of them begin at least from a shared moral attitude.

Differences among Machiavels and tool villains emerge when we compare later with earlier versions, for the later ones are more highly individualized and psychologized and the nature of their relationship is far more subtly presented. Richard and Buckingham in Richard III, for example, are more complex and unpredictable creations than Lorenzo and Pedringano in The Spanish Tragedy, or Barabas and Ithamore in The Jew of Malta. Buckingham is falsely encouraged to think that his advice and friendship are essential to Richard when, in fact, Richard is always the guiding spirit who has feelings for no one. And the changing nature of their relationship is closely tied to the movement of the plot. The murder of the princes in the Tower, for instance, is clearly established as the turning point of the action since it becomes the issue over which the two men begin to acknowledge their differences. Moreover, the ironies here are not offered simply as a bit of delicious humor; they are woven into the overall design of the play. Indeed, to provide a greater sense of integration and unity to the action and to point up the ironic aspects of the plotting, the sources have been altered, adding the vituperative Queen Margaret, who even predicts Buckingham's fate upon his very first appearance.

In the course of his career, Shakespeare presents several examples of the Machiavel and the tool villain. Among the most interesting of the latter is Camillo, who might be called the tool villain manqué of The Winter's Tale. By refusing to act as an agent for the jealous Leontes, in effect serving as his tool villain, Camillo ultimately helps bring about the repentant king's reunion with his lost wife and daughter.

But the Jacobean theater produced versions of these type characters who are far more extreme and unusual. The Machiavels in Webster's *The Duchess of Malfi*, for instance, are no longer motivated by the customary drive for power and wealth found in earlier examples. Instead, neither we nor they can be quite sure what it is the two brothers hope to gain by forbidding their sister's remarriage. We can only judge how intensely they are determined to govern her behavior by the cruelty of their conduct toward her. And as the relationship of Machiavel to victim has altered, so, too, has the relationship of tool villain and victim. In this case, Bosola, employed as an agent of her brothers, attempts to use the Duchess to prove that his cynical view of human nature is correct. But gradually won over by her dignity and courage, he becomes not simply her executioner but her revenger. His victim serves as a kind of example for him, and the play traces his growing recognition of her true worth. The tool villain has become the central character of the work and the real focus of our attention. Rather than functioning simply as the base second means of the Machiavel, the tool villain is now the protagonist; his involvement and reactions are at the heart of the matter. In earlier drama the force of the moral code was demonstrated by the fate of the Machiavel and the tool villain; now it is being challenged, questioned, and tested.

The relationship of Machiavel and tool villain receives still a different treatment in Middleton and Rowley's *The Changeling*. Here the services of the tool villain DeFlores are to be rewarded not with money or position – he refuses his employer's 3,000 florins – but rather with love. In fact, the tool villain is so enamoured of the woman who hires his services that he will help her marry another so long as he can share her bed. And what is even more fascinating, the action of the play then dramatizes the depth and commitment of the tool villain's affection and the growing appreciation of this love by the one who loathed him at the start. In addition, we come to recognize the obtuseness of the young woman who can so easily adjust the moral code to justify her own conduct. In a perverse manner, the tool villain has actually become a kind of hero, admirable for the strength, courage, and honesty of his affection, and the woman cast as Machiavel, who earlier defied the moral code, only begins to understand the extent of her criminality as she dies.

In sum, both Jacobean tragedies illustrate aspects of these type characters we have not seen before. First, the admirable traits found in Bosola and DeFlores are qualities unknown to earlier examples of the tool villain. Realizing at last how wrong he was, Bosola repents and tries to comfort the woman he has just strangled:

> What would I do, were this to do again?
> I would not change my peace of conscience
> For all the wealth of Europe. She stirs; here's life.
> Return, fair soul, from darkness, and lead mine
> Out of this sensible hell. (IV.ii.339–343)

DeFlores, too, warns Beatrice-Joanna that his devotion to her is so strong

'my life I rate at nothing' (III.iv.); taking precedent over all other considerations, his love is so intense that he will sacrifice everything for her. Although his feelings lead him to commit terrible deeds, his total dedication
makes him oddly sympathetic.

Along with this change in the tool villain, the nature of the Machiavel
has metamorphosed as well. Earlier incarnations of this type character,
seeking the traditional goals of wealth or power, have been replaced by
figures who are driven just as intensely but by deeper private and idio-
syncratic emotions – indeed, in some cases the passions are so pathologi-
cal that we cannot quite grasp their true nature. The individualized
personality of the earlier Machiavel, whose ambitions were carefully integrated into the plotting of the action and whose rewards and punishments
reflected the belief that the universe was somehow morally responsive,
has yielded to criminals of a psychotic nature who torment one another in
a world governed by meaningless chance, or who discover that the line
between hatred and love is sometimes hard to find. The conclusion reinforces the pointlessness of human endeavor and the inanity of expecting an ordered, or rational, or moral universe. The person Bosola wants
most to help is the man he mistakenly murders in the darkness:

> The man I would have saved 'bove mine own life!
> We are merely the stars' tennis balls, struck and banded
> Which way please them. (V.iv.53–55)

Despite her loathing for him and what he recognizes as the pettiness and
selfishness of her nature, DeFlores 'cannot choose but love' Beatrice-
Joanna. In this drama, the ways of individuals, like their fates, lie beyond
reason.

The shrew, the last type character we considered, demonstrates changes
in the conception of the roles of husband and wife. The relationship
established betwen Katherine and Petruchio in Shakespeare's The Taming of
the Shrew, the notion of the proper place of women in marriage, is unlike
that in the two plays that are versions of this work. Katherine in The Shrew is
not portrayed as morally or intellectually inferior to men, nor does she
need to be thoroughly submissive and subservient to her husband. The
reformed heroine of A Shrew, in contrast, emphasizes her heritage as a
descendent of Eve, the source of sin and death: the descendant of Eve can
only abase herself, laying her hands under her husband's feet 'to tread.'
But Katherine in The Shrew develops the analogy between domesticity and
politics: the wife is to the husband as the subject is to the prince. The
mutual concern, trust, and love that are essential to a successful marriage
are also demonstrated between subject and prince in the ideal commonwealth. In both cases, mutually beneficial aims are the consequence of a
shared sense of responsibility for happiness and peace.

Despite her unconformity, Shakespeare's Katherine is not indifferent to
public opinion. Her surprising sensitivity to commonly held notions of

propriety and to such matters as her reputation enable us to understand the course of her development. Moreover, since Petruchio is a perfect match for her in wit and intelligence as well as in spirit, inventiveness, brashness, and even shrewishness, we expect that ultimately each of these characters will come to love one another. The play then dramatizes how so very obstinate a woman as Katherine can bring herself to admit, both to herself and to others, that her happiness lies in her husband's happiness as his does in hers.

In the sequel to the Shakespearean play, John Fletcher's heroine, Maria, also seems to be out to prove that husbands and wives must regard each other with 'due equality' to find happiness in marriage. Surprisingly enough, her husband seems to agree, for Petruchio demands neither service nor obedience. Yet Maria subjects her bridegroom to a series of unpleasant demonstrations of her willfulness, evidently simply to show her power. And both of them discuss the matter of consummating their marriage in coarse language with threats of punishment, adultery, and cuckoldry. The reasons for the happy resolution are unclear and un-related to the prior action: Maria, having thoroughly beaten and frustrated her husband, finally yields him a dominance that is more than he ever sought and, perhaps, more than seems consistent with their happiness. But nowhere do we come to understand how these two have learned the need for mutual concern, trust, and love which can sustain their marriage.

The type characters of Renaissance drama help us to gauge changes in public opinion since differences in the presentation and treatment of these characters are a consequence of the ways in which issues and atti-tudes in contemporary society crystallized around them. In effect, these characters, who appear repeatedly in the plays of this period, provide us with a useful means of determining in what ways the drama at the end of the sixteenth century confronted, or failed to confront, the problems faced by society – such questions as how we define civilization and what are its virtues, what are the proper ambitions for the good life, or what models of conduct are suitable for the politician.

What emerges from our analysis is not new but perhaps is not always recognized with quite so much clarity. We must be impressed by the extent and rapidity of the changes in social attitudes during the years from 1585 to 1620. As a popular public form, Renaissance drama reflects an astonishing evolution in morals and values. The conservative outlook of the Elizabethan court seems to have begun to grow more free, offering more of a challenge to tradition, even before the old Queen died and her nephew set the style and tone of the age that was to bear his name. When he finally arrived on the throne, the winds of change had already begun to gather force. The growing power of the Commons, the constant squabb-ling over religions and rituals, the economic upheaval that affected both urban and rural life, together with the manners and taste set by the new monarchy, all contributed to the intensity and pervasiveness of what England experienced in the first decade of the seventeenth century.

Perhaps a final observation about type characters is in order. That several of them, so popular at the turn of the century, become much less prominent in the drama after 1620 indicates not that they are unimportant but rather that the social and moral questions they raised had become unimportant. From their original incarnations they metamorphosed into the independent wives and rakish courtiers of Restoration comedy, into the superhuman heroes of Restoration tragedy, into the conniving villains of nineteenth-century melodrama, and into those savage or evil forces of the antimasque who are dispelled by the arrival of the Jacobean court in all its glory. At long last those powerful winds of change had fundamentally altered not only the landscape but its population.

Bibliography

Allen, J. W. *A History of Political Thought in the Sixteenth Century*. New York: Barnes and Noble, 1960.

Anon. *Robin Goodfellow: His Mad Pranks and Merry Jests*. London, 1628.

Ariosto, Ludovico. *Orlando Furioso*, translated by Sir John Harington, selected and edited by Rudolf Gottfried. Bloomington: Indiana University Press, 1969.

Arthos, John. *On The Poetry of Spenser and the Form of Romances*. London: Allen and Unwin, 1956.

Babb, Lawrence. *The Elizabethan Malady*. East Lansing: Michigan State University Press, 1956.

Bakeless, John. *Christopher Marlowe: The Man in His Time*. New York: William Morrow, 1937.

Ball, Robert Hamilton. *The Amazing Career of Sir Giles Overreach*. Princeton: University Press, 1939.

Barker, Gerald. 'Themes and Variations in Shakespeare's *Pericles*.' *English Studies* (1963), 44:401–444.

Barroll, J. Leeds. *Artificial Persons The Formation of Character in the Tragedies of Shakespeare*. Columbia: University of South Carolina Press, 1974.

Battenhouse, Roy W. *Marlowe's Tamburlaine: A Study in Renaissance Moral Philosophy*. Nashville: Vanderbilt University Press, 1941.

Bean, John C. 'Comic Structure and the Humanizing of Kate in *The Taming of the Shrew*.' *The Woman's Part*, edited by Carol Lenz, *et al*. Urbana: University of Illinois Press, 1980.

Bentley, Eric. *The Life of The Drama*. New York: Atheneum, 1964.

Bergeron, David M. *Shakespeare's Romances and the Royal Family*. Lawrence: University of Kansas Press, 1985.

Bernheimer, Richard. *Wild Men in the Middle Ages*. Cambridge: Harvard University Press, 1952.

Boughner, Daniel C. *The Braggart in Renaissance Comedy*. Minneapolis: The University of Minnesota Press, 1954.

Bowers, Fredson, Thayer. 'Kyd's Pedringano: Sources and Parallels,' *Harvard Studies and Notes in Philology and Literature* (1931), 13:241–249.

Bradbrook, M. C. 'Dramatic Role as Social Image, a study of *The Taming of the Shrew*.' *Shakespeare Jahrbuch* (1958), 132–50.

Bradbrook, M. C. *Themes and Conventions of Elizabethan Tragedy*. Cambridge: University Press, 1960.

Brooke, Nicholas. *Horrid Laughter in Jacobean Tragedy*. London: Open Books, 1979.

Bryan, Margaret B. 'Sir Walter Blunt. There's Honor for You!' *Shakespeare Quarterly* (1975), 26:292–298.

Bryant, J. A., Jr. *The Compassionate Satirist Ben Jonson and His Imperfect World*. Athens: University of Georgia Press, 1972.

Bullough, Geoffrey, ed. *Narrative and Dramatic Sources of Shakespeare*. 4 vols. New York: Columbia University Press, 1957–1975.

Calvin, John. *Institutes*, translated by F. L. Battles and edited by John T. McNeil. Philadelphia: Westminister Press, 1960

Calvin, John. *Institutes of the Christian Religion*, translated by John Allen. Philadelphia, 1928.

Castiglione, Baldassare. *The Book of the Courtier*, translated by Sir Thomas Hoby. New York: Dutton, 1966.

Certain Sermons or Homilies appointed to be read in Churches. Oxford, 1844.

Chambers, E. K. *Elizabethan Stage*. 4 volumes. Oxford: The Clarendon Press, 1966.

Cheney, Donald. *Spenser's Image of Nature: Wild Man and Shepherd in The Fairie Queene*. New Haven: Yale University Press, 1966.

Cole, Douglas. 'The Comic Accomplice in Elizabethan Revenge Tragedy,' *Renaissance Drama IX* (1966), 125–139.

Cole, Douglas. *Suffering and Evil in the Plays of Christopher Marlowe*. Princeton: University Press, 1962.

Colie, Rosalie. *Shakespeare's Living Art*. Princeton: University Press, 1974.

Corfield, Cosmo. 'Why Does Prospero Abjure His "Rough Magic"?' *Shakespeare Quarterly* (1985), 36:31–48.

Council, Norman. *When Honour's At the Stake*. London: Allen and Unwin, 1973.

Craig, Hardin. *The Enchanted Glass*. New York: Oxford University Press, 1952.

Cullen, Patrick. *Spenser, Marvell, and Renaissance Poetry*. Cambridge: Harvard University Press, 1970.

Dash, Irene G. *Wooing, Wedding, and Power*. New York: Columbia University Press, 1981.

Davis, Walter R. *Sidney's Arcadia*. New Haven: Yale University Press, 1965.

Dessen, Alan C. *Jonson's Moral Comedy*. Evanston: Northwestern University Press, 1971.

Dickson, Arthur. *Valentine and Orson, A Study in Late Medieval Romance*. New York: Columbia University Press, 1929.

Dollimore, Jonathan and Alan Sinfield, eds. *Political Shakespeare*. Ithaca: Cornell University Press, 1985.

Dusinberre, Juliet. *Shakespeare and the Nature of Women*. New York: Barnes and Noble, 1975.

Edwards, Philip, Inga-Stina Ewbank, and G. K. Hunter. *Shakespeare's Styles*. Cambridge: Cambridge University Press, 1980.

Ellis-Fermor, Una. *The Jacobean Drama*. New York: Vintage Books, 1964.

Elyot, Sir Thomas. *The Boke Named the Governour*, edited by Henry Herbert Stephen Croft. 2 vols. London: Kegan Paul, Trench, and Co., 1883.

Empson, William. *Some Versions of Pastoral*. London: Chatto and Windus, 1950.

Enck, John J. *Jonson and the Comic Truth*. Madison: The University of Wisconsin Press, 1966.

Farr, Dorothy M. *Thomas Middleton and the Drama of Realism*. New York: Barnes and Noble, 1973.

Felperin, Howard. *Shakespearean Romance*. Princeton: University Press, 1972.

Fortescue, G. W. 'The Soldier,' in *Shakespeare's England*, edited by Sir Walter Raleigh, *et. al.* Vol. IV. Oxford: Clarendon Press, 1917.

French, Marilyn. *Shakespeare's Division of Experience*. New York: Summit Books, 1981.

Frey, Charles. 'The Tempest and the New World.' *Shakespeare Quarterly* (1979), 30:29–41.

Frye, Northrop. *Anatomy of Criticism*. Princeton: University Press, 1957.

Frost, David L. *The School of Shakespeare*. Cambridge: University Press, 1968.

Garber, Marjorie. *The Coming of Age in Shakespeare*. New York: Methuen, 1981.

Gellert, Bridget J. *Voices of Melancholy Studies in Literary Treatments of Melancholy in Renaissance England*. New York: Barnes and Noble, 1971.

Gibbons, Brian *Jacobean City Comedy*. London: Rupert Hart-Davis, 1968.

Greenblatt, Stephen. *Renaissance Self-Fashioning From More to Shakespeare*. Chicago: University of Chicago Press, 1980.

Hankins, John E. 'Caliban and the Natural Man.' *PMLA* (1947), 62:793–801.

Harbage, Alfred. *The Annals of English Drama*, revised by S. Schoenbaum. London: Methuen & Co., 1964.

Haydn, Hiram. *The Counter-Renaissance*. New York: Grove Press, 1950.

Henslowe, Philip. *Henslowe's Diary*, edited by R. A. Foakes and R. T. Rickert. Cambridge: University Press, 1961.

Hoeniger, F. D. and Thomas Edwards. 'An Approach to the Problem of Pericles.' *Shakespeare Survey* (1952), 5:25–49.

Hooker, Richard. *Of the Laws of Ecclesiastical Polity*. 2 vols. London: J. M. Dent & Sons, 1960.

Hosley, Richard. 'Sources and Analogues of The Taming of the Shrew.' *Huntington Library Quarterly* (1963–64), 27:289–308.

Hoy, Cyrus. 'Fletcherian Romantic Comedy.' *Research Opportunities in Renaissance Drama* (1984), 27:3–11.

Hunter, G. K. 'Bourgeois comedy: Shakespeare and Dekker,' *Shakespeare and his contemporaries*, ed. E. A. J. Honigmann. Manchester: Manchester University Press, 1986.

Hunter, G. K. *John Lyly The Humanist as Courtier*. London: Routledge, Kegan Paul, 1962.

Hunter, Robert Grams. *Shakespeare and the Comedy of Forgiveness*. New York: Columbia University Press, 1965.

Jackson, Gabriele Bernhard. *Vision and Judgment in Ben Jonson's Drama*. New Haven: Yale University Press, 1968.

James, D. G. *The Dream of Prospero*. Oxford: University Press, 1967.

Jardine, Lisa. *Still Harping on Daughters*. Totowa: Barnes and Noble, 1983.

Jones, Emrys. *The Origins of Shakespeare*. Oxford: University Press, 1977.

Jones, Emrys. *Scenic Form in Shakespeare*. New York: Oxford University Press, 1985.

Jorgensen, P. A. 'Military Rank in Shakespeare,' HLQ, 14 (1950), I:17–41.

Kahn, Coppelia. 'The Taming of the Shrew: Shakespeare's Mirror of Marriage.' *Modern Language Studies* (1975), 5:88–102.

Kaplan, Joel H. 'Virtue's Holiday: Thomas Dekker and Simon Eyre,' *Renaissance Drama* N.S. II (1969), 103–122.

Kelso, Ruth. *The Doctrine of the English Gentleman in the Sixteenth Century*. Urbana: University of Illinois Press, 1929.

Kocher, Paul H. *Christopher Marlowe: A Study of His Thought, Learning, and Character*. New York: Chapel Hill: University of North Carolina Press, 1946.

Leech, Clifford. 'The Structure of Tamburlaine.' *Tulane Drama Review* (1946), 4:32–46.

Leggatt, Alexander. *Ben Jonson His Vision and His Art*. New York: Methuen, 1981.

Leggatt, Alexander. *Citizen Comedy in the Age of Shakespeare*. Toronto: University of Toronto Press, 1973.

Levin, Harry. *The Overreacher*. Cambridge: Harvard University Press, 1952.

Levin, Richard. *The Multiple Plot in English Renaissance Drama*. Chicago: University of Chicago Press, 1971.

Lewis, Wyndham. *The Lion and The Fox*. New York: Barnes and Noble, n.d.

Lockyer, Roger. *Buckingham, The Life and Political Career of George Villiers*. London: Longman, 1981.

Mack, Maynard. *King Lear in Our Time*. Berkeley: University of California Press, 1965.

Mahood, M. M. *Poetry and Humanism*. London: Jonathan Cape, 1950.

McElroy, Bernard. *Shakespeare's Mature Tragedies*. Princeton: University Press, 1973.

Mirandola, Gianfrancesco Pico Della. *Oration on the Dignity of Man*, translated by Elizabeth Livermore Forbes in *The Renaissance Philosophy of Man*, edited by Ernst Cassirer, *et al*. Chicago: University of Chicago Press, 1948.

Montaigne, Michel. *The Third Book of Essais*, translated by J. M. Cohen. Baltimore: Penguin Books, 1958.

Mortenson, Peter. 'The Economics of Joy in The Shoemaker's Holiday,' SEL (1976), 16:241–252.

Muir, Kenneth. *Shakespeare as Collaborator*. New York: Barnes and Noble, 1960.

Nohanberg, James. *The Analogy of The Fairie Queene*. Princeton: University Press, 1976.

Parrot, Henry. *VIII Cures for the Itch: Characters, Epigrams, Epitaphs*. London, 1626.

Partridge, Edward B. *The Broken Compass: A Study of the Major Comedies of Ben Jonson*. New York: Columbia University Press, 1958.

Patericke, Simon. *A Discourse Upon the Meanes of Wel Governing and ... Against Nicholas Machiavel the Florentine*. London, 1608.

Paylor, W. J., ed. *The Overburian Characters by Sir Thomas Overbury*. Oxford: The Percy Reprints No., XIII, 1936.

Pearce, Roy Harvey. 'Primitivistic Ideas in *The Faerie Queene*.' JEGP (1945), 44:139–151.

Pearson, Lu Emily. *Elizabethans at Home*. Stanford: University Press, 1957.

Perkins, William. *Works*. Cambridge, 1603.

Pettet, E. C. *Shakespeare and the Romance Tradition*. London: Staples Press, 1949.

Pinciss, Gerald. *Christopher Marlowe*. New York: Frederick Ungar, 1975.

Praz, Mario. 'Machiavelli and the Elizabethans,' *Proceedings of the British Academy* XIII (1928).

Raab, F. *The English Face of Machiavelli*. London: Routledge and Kegan Paul, 1964.

Raleigh, Sir Walter. *The Complete Works*, edited by Oldys and Birch. Oxford: University Press, 1829.

Ranald, Margaret Loftus. 'The Manning of the Haggard; or, *The Taming of the Shrew* .' *Essays in Literature* (1974), 1:149–165.

Ribner, Irving. 'The Idea of History in Marlowe's *Tamburlaine*.' JEGP (1953), 20:251–266.

Rosier, James. *True Relation of the Most Prosperous Voyage ... in ... the Land of Virginia*. London, 1605.

Rozett, Martha Tuck. *The Doctrine of Election and the Emergence of Elizabethan Tragedy*. Princeton: University Press, 1984.

Saccio, Peter. *The Court Comedies of John Lyly*. Princeton: University Press, 1969.

Salingar, L. G. 'The Elizabethan Literary Renaissance,' in *The Age of Shakespeare*, edited by Boris Ford. Harmondsworth: Penguin Books, 1982.

Sanders, Wilbur. *The Dramatist and the Received Idea*. Cambridge: University Press, 1968.

The Second Tome of Homilies. London, 1587.

Shepherd, Simon. *Amazons and Warrior Women*. New York: St Martin's Press, 1981.

Sidney, Sir Philip. *An Apology for Poetry*, edited by Geoffrey Shepherd. London: Thomas Nelson and Sons, 1965.

Sinfield, Alan. *Literature in Protestant England 1560–1660*. Totowa: Barnes and Noble Books, 1983.

Smith, Henry. *A Preparative to Marriage*. London, 1591.

Smith, John. *The Generall Historie of Virginia, New England and The Summer Isles*. London, 1624.

Spivack, Bernard. *Shakespeare and the Allegory of Evil*. New York: Columbia University Press, 1958.

Steane, J. B. *Marlowe: A Critical Study*. Cambridge: University Press, 1965.

Summers, Joseph H. *Dreams of Love and Power*. Oxford: Clarendon Press, 1984.

Sweeny, John Gordon III. *Jonson and the Psychology of Public Theater*. Princeton: University Press, 1985.

Tayler, Edward William. *Nature and Art in Renaissance Literature*. New York: Columbia University Press, 1964.

Tillyard, E. M. W. *Shakespeare's History Plays*. New York: Macmillan, 1944.

Tolliver, Harold. *Pastoral Forms and Attitudes*. Berkeley: University of California Press, 1971.

Tomlinson, T. B. *A Study of Elizabethan and Jacobean Tragedy*. Cambridge: University Press, 1964.

Tonkin, Humphrey. *Spenser's Courteous Pastoral*. Oxford: University Press, 1972.

Turberville, George. *The Book of Faulconrie or Hawking*. London, 1575.

Waith, Eugene M. *The Herculean Hero in Marlowe, Chapman, Shakespeare, and Dryden*. New York: Columbia University Press, 1962.

Watson, Curtis Brown. *Shakespeare and the Renaissance Concept of Honor*. Princeton: University Press, 1960.

White, Hayden. 'The Forms of Wildness: Archaeology of an Idea,' in *The Wild Man Within*, ed. Edward Dudley and Maxmillian Novak. Pittsburgh: University of Pittsburgh Press, 1972.

Woodbridge, Linda. *Women and the English Renaissance*. Urbana: University of Illinois Press, 1984.

Wright, Louis B. *Middle-Class Culture in Elizabethan England*. Chapel Hill: University of North Carolina Press, 1935.

Young, David. *The Heart's Forest*. New Haven: Yale University Press, 1972.

Young David. *Something of Great Constancy: The Art of A Midsummer Night's Dream*. New Haven: Yale University Press, 1966.

Editions of Plays

Anon. *Mucedorus*, edited by Norman Rabkin in *Drama of the English Renaissance*, Vol. I., edited by Russell Fraser and Norman Rabkin. New York: Macmillan Publishing Co., 1976.

Dekker, Thomas. *The Shoemaker's Holiday*, edited by R. L. Smallwood and Stanley Wells. Baltimore: The Johns Hopkins Press, 1979.

Fletcher, John. *The Woman's Prize or The Tamer Tam'd* in *The Dramatic Works in the Beaumont and Fletcher Canon*, general editor Fredson Bowers. Vol. IV. Cambridge: University Press, 1979.

Fletcher, John. *The Woman's Prize or The Tamer Tamed: A Critical Edition* by George B. Ferguson. The Hague: Mouton, 1966.

Greene, Robert. *Orlando Furioso*. Malone Society Reprints. Oxford University Press, 1907.

Jonson, Ben. *Works* edited by C. H. Herford and Percy Simpson Oxford: Clarendon Press, 1925–52.

Jonson, Benjamin. *The Alchemist*, ed. by Alvin B. Yale University Press, 1974.

Kyd, Thomas. *The Spanish Tragedy*, edited by Philip Edwards. Cambridge: Harvard University Press, 1959.

Lyly, John. *Campaspe*, in *Chief Pre-Shakespearean Dramas*, edited by Joseph Quincy Adams. Cambridge: Houghton Mifflin Co., 1924.

Marlowe, Christopher. *Doctor Faustus*, edited by John D. Jump. Cambridge: Harvard University Press, 1962.

Marlowe, Christopher. *Tamburlaine the Great*, edited by J. S. Cunningham. Baltimore: Johns Hopkins Press, 1981.

Marlowe, Christopher. *The Jew of Malta*, edited by N. W. Bawcutt. Baltimore: The Johns Hopkins University Press, 1978.

Massinger, Philip. *The Plays and Poems of*, edited by Philip Edwards and Colin Gibson. Oxford: University Press, 1976.

Massinger, Philip. *A New Way to Pay Old Debts*, in *Drama of the English Renaissance*, Vol. II., edited by Rusell Fraser and Norman Rabkin. New York: Macmillan Publishing Co., 1976.

Middleton, Thomas and William Rowley. *The Changeling*, edited by N. W. Bawcutt. Cambridge: Harvard University Press, 1961.

Shakespeare, William. *A Midsummer Night's Dream*, edited by R. A. Foakes. Cambridge: University Press, 1984.

Shakespeare, William. *Cymbeline*, edited by James Nosworthy. London: Methuen and Co., 1966.

Shakespeare, William. *King Henry IV, Part One*, edited by A. R. Humphreys. London: Methuen and Co., 1965.

Shakespeare, William. *King Lear*, edited by Kenneth Muir. Cambridge: Harvard University Press, 1959.

Shakespeare, William. *King Richard III*, edited by Antony Hammond. London: Methuen and Co., 1981.

Shakespeare, William. *Much Ado About Nothing*, edited by A. R. Humphreys. London: Methuen and Co., 1981.

Shakespeare, William. *Pericles*, edited by F. D. Hoeniger. London: Methuen and Co., 1963.

Shakespeare, William. *The Taming of the Shrew*, edited by George Hibbard. New York: New Penguin, 1968.

Shakespeare, William. *The Taming of the Shrew*, edited by Brian Morris. London: Methuen and Co., 1981.

Shakespeare, William. *The Taming of the Shrew*, edited by H. J. Oliver. New York: Oxford University Press, 1984.

Shakespeare, William. *The Tempest*, edited by Frank Kermode. Cambridge: Harvard University Press, 1958.

Webster, John. *The Duchess of Malfi*, edited by John Russell Brown. London: Methuen and Co., 1964.

Index